SPIES
of MISSISSIPPI

SPIES
of MISSISSIPPI

THE TRUE STORY OF
THE SPY NETWORK THAT TRIED TO DESTROY THE
CIVIL RIGHTS MOVEMENT

Rick Bowers

NATIONAL GEOGRAPHIC

WASHINGTON, D.C.

The National Geographic Society is one of the world's largest nonprofit scientific
and educational organizations. Founded in 1888 to "increase and diffuse
geographic knowledge," the Society works to inspire people to care about the
planet. It reaches more than 325 million people worldwide each month through
its official journal, *National Geographic,* and other magazines; National Geographic
Channel; television documentaries; music; radio; films; books; DVDs; maps;
exhibitions; school publishing programs; interactive media; and merchandise.
National Geographic has funded more than 9,000 scientific research, conservation
and exploration projects and supports an education program combating
geographic illiteracy. For more information, visit nationalgeographic.com.

For more information, please call 1-800-NGS LINE (647-5463)
or write to the following address:
National Geographic Society
1145 17th Street N.W.
Washington, D.C. 20036-4688 U.S.A.

Visit us online at www.nationalgeographic.com/books

For librarians and teachers: www.ngchildrensbooks.org

More for kids from National Geographic: kids.nationalgeographic.com

For information about special discounts for bulk purchases, please contact
National Geographic Books Special Sales: ngspecsales@ngs.org

For rights or permissions inquiries, please contact National Geographic Books
Subsidiary Rights: ngbookrights@ngs.org

Trade hardcover ISBN: 978-1-4263-0595-5
Reinforced Library Edition ISBN: 978-1-4263-0596-2

Printed in the United States of America

Table of Contents

Prologue

Twelve of the most powerful men in the state controlled a secretive network of spies and informants.

A cadre of covert operatives used code names like Agent X, Agent Y, and Agent Zero.

Neighbors spied on neighbors. Teachers spied on students. Ministers spied on churchgoers. Spies spied on spies.

This is not the description of a Cold War–era secret police force or a futuristic sci-fi dictatorship. This government-run spy network infiltrated the lives of private citizens right here in the United States and not too long ago—in the state of Mississippi during the height of the civil rights movement of the 1950s and '60s.

The Mississippi State Sovereignty Commission operated as a clandestine investigative arm of the state government for more than a decade, compiling secret files on more than 87,000 private citizens and organizations.

Staffed by a team of professional agents, including former FBI agents police investigators, and private detectives the Commission had a fundamental mission: to save segregation at all costs. In the process, its agents carried out the most extensive state spying program in U.S. history.

How do we know all this is true? The Commission itself tells us. The 134,000 pages in its once-secret investigative file tell the story of its clandestine programs, its network of neighborhood informants, its brutal behind-the-scenes maneuvering, and its intervention in many of the most historically significant events of the civil rights era.

For this book, I've filled out the story with oral histories, personal memoirs, historical studies, academic dissertations, government documents, and newspaper and magazine articles from the era. In addition, I've traveled across Mississippi— from the cotton fields in the Mississippi River Delta to the beach towns on the Gulf Coast to the capital of Jackson—interviewing people connected to the story. I've also uncovered surveillance documents and photographs, including a hand-drawn map showing the burial site of three murdered civil rights workers and photos of student protestors with red numbers scrawled next to their faces. Those numbers targeted the "subversives" for further investigation.

Despite the tracks left behind by the anti–civil rights spies and the excellent research and writing on the subject in Mississippi, the story remains largely unknown to the general public, usually relegated to a footnote in the history of the civil rights movement.

No longer.

This is how it happened.

The Genesis

At noon sharp on a bright, 43-degree day in January of 1956, J. P. Coleman placed his right hand on his mother's Bible and took the oath to become the 51st governor of Mississippi. The 6-foot-2-inch gentleman farmer, lawyer, and Civil War historian cast an impressive figure as he stood at the podium preparing to deliver his inaugural address. Coleman looked out over the 3,000 people gathered in the public square in the state capital of Jackson. Virtually all the faces looking back at him were white.

A segregationist and skilled public speaker, Coleman launched into his inaugural address, vowing to "maintain the separation of the white and Negro races." But aware that tensions between whites and blacks were threatening to flare into violence in a number of cities and towns across the state, Coleman also warned his audience—including both chambers of the state legislature and the state supreme court—that preserving segregation was "no task for the amateur or the hothead." When it came to the tense relationship between whites and blacks in Mississippi, Coleman wanted "peace and quiet." In Mississippi in 1956, that made him a moderate.

Once settled into the governor's mansion, Coleman waded through a stream of bills coming to his desk from the state legislature, which was fixated on shoring up the walls of segregation. House Bill 880 caught his eye. It called for the creation of the Mississippi State Sovereignty Commission, a special agency that would preserve the state's "sovereignty"—that is, its right to govern itself without undue interference from the federal government or private pressure groups. The lawmakers behind the bill had made it clear that sovereignty was really just a high-minded code word for segregation, the official state policy of keeping the races separate and keeping whites in a position of power over blacks. The Commission would be granted extraordinary powers, including the power to investigate private citizens and organizations, maintain secret files, force witnesses to testify, and even make arrests.

From a legal standpoint, Coleman worried that such a potent and secretive investigative agency could trample on the rights of private citizens. From a political stand-point, he knew that those powerful lawmakers would not back down until the bill was signed into law. And from a practical standpoint, he had to admit that having his own operatives to keep an eye on civil rights "agitators" could help to maintain his coveted racial peace and quiet. So the new governor signed the bill, vowing to contain the agency's power by surrounding it with moderates like him, instead of the outspoken, racist politicians and civic leaders he called "fire-eaters." With the stroke of his pen, the Commission was born. Governor Coleman, despite his reluctance, became the overseer of the state's new segregation watchdogs.

Growing Outrage, Growing Backlash

The segregation watchdogs would have plenty to keep an eye on. From Gulfport to Greenville, civil rights activists had stepped up their boycotts, marches, prayer vigils, and demonstrations against segregation and discrimination, inequality and injustice. The catalyst had been the 1954 U.S. Supreme Court ruling in *Brown v. Board of Education*, which barred segregation in public schools, requiring states to integrate schools "with all deliberate speed." The ruling prompted more and more opponents of segregation to join the NAACP, an interracial organization formed in 1909 to advocate for equal rights for African Americans. Now the NAACP was setting up local chapters in cities and towns throughout Mississippi—and the rest of the country—to push for integration.

The growing outrage of blacks was greeted with a growing backlash from many whites. The more extreme opponents of integration called for a campaign of "massive resistance" by white community leaders and ordinary citizens. City leaders barred demonstrations; county sheriffs began jailing activists on trumped-up charges; the Ku Klux Klan awoke from a long slumber with cross burnings, beatings, and even murder.

Thousands of people were joining the newly formed White Citizens' Council, a self-described civic organization with a stated mission of defending segregation by legal means—and without violence. The movement was launched by Mississippi Circuit Court Judge Thomas Pickens Brady, who published a handbook entitled *Black Monday*, denouncing the 1954 Supreme Court ruling and spelling out the group's core beliefs. Brady called for the disbandment of the NAACP and proposed radical alternatives to integrated schools, including the abolition of all public schools and even the creation of a separate state for Negroes.

By the time Governor Coleman took office, the state was studded with Council chapters. Their leaders saturated their community newspapers with pro-segregation messages, advocated for tougher segregation ordinances, supported segregationist political candidates, and fiercely denounced the NAACP, calling it the "National Association for the Agitation of Colored People." The Council's most effective weapon was the economic advantage that middle and upper class whites held over the majority of blacks. Council leaders got suspected civil rights sympathizers fired from their jobs, turned down for credit, forced out of business, or evicted from their homes. Behind the scenes, more than a few Council leaders resorted to threats, intimidation, and violence, working hand-in-hand with the Klan. Critics of the White Citizens' Council—noting that its leaders were usually respected white businessmen dressed in suits and ties rather than hoods and robes, dubbed the organization "The Country Club Klan."

—o

Most black Mississippians were not buying segregation, even if their views had to be kept to low whispers to avoid persecution. Many others were voting with their feet by moving North in search of better jobs and more tolerance. Still others, convinced that the entrenched white political class would never give up power, chose to make the best of it in a black-and-white world. Those few subservient blacks who played up to white authority figures in exchange for preferential treatment were branded "Uncle Toms," a term drawn from a fictional character in Harriet Beecher Stowe's novel *Uncle Tom's Cabin*. The term was a badge of shame in the black community, suggesting that the person was selling out his or her own people.

The Mississippi State Sovereignty Commission was counting on it.

The Bible

As the tension between the races simmered, Governor
Coleman assumed the chairmanship of the board that
would oversee the Sovereignty Commission. The 12
board members—including the powerful president of the
Mississippi Senate, speaker of the Mississippi House, and
state attorney general—would provide political cover for
the agency's hidden operations. Once the board was in
place, Coleman set up a propaganda unit to wage a war of
words against the NAACP. The unit would produce and
distribute pro-segregation messages, ultimately compiling
a package of press releases, films, speeches, and testimo-
nials that would become known as "The 'Bible.'"

Coleman appointed his former campaign publicity chief
Hal DeCell to head up the unit. DeCell, editor of the weekly
Deer Creek *Pilot* in the tiny delta town of Twin Forks,
had lobbied for a big public relations job with the state,
promising to combat the "vicious falsehoods" slung by civil

rights groups, the federal government, and the "poison pens" of the elite Northern press. As public relations chief, DeCell began crafting the storyline that segregation was good for both whites and blacks, and that most "Negroes" in the Magnolia State actually preferred it. He started sending pro-segregation editorials to newspapers across the country, developing a pro-segregation film, and distributing pamphlets that painted a glowing portrait of race relations in the state. DeCell escorted Northern newspaper editors on tours of the Mississippi River and excursions to the tourist towns on the Gulf, trying to show that whites and blacks lived and worked in carefully controlled harmony in segregated Mississippi.

—o

As would be expected, DeCell's public relations package did not mention the state's long history of maintaining white dominance over blacks, which dated back to the earliest days of slavery. At that time the state established rigid "slave codes" that defined African Americans as property, dictated the conditions of their captivity, and prescribed brutal punishments for the slightest infractions. Even after the Civil War and the abolition of slavery, the ruling class in Mississippi—and throughout the South—retained power, establishing new laws, customs, and punishments that bore a striking resemblance to the old slave codes.

The new "black codes" restricted freedom of speech, freedom of travel, freedom to vote, to own land, or to choose an occupation. "White supremacy"—the concept that white people were naturally superior to blacks—was written into law, taught in schools, praised in churches, and reinforced in the media. The laws and customs that propped up white power were commonly referred to as Jim Crow, after an old, crippled black character portrayed by white minstrel show performers. With their faces blackened by charcoal or burnt cork, the minstrel show-men danced a ridiculous jig and sang a mocking song titled "Jump Jim Crow," inadvertently putting a name to the degrading conditions that dominated the lives of African Americans.

The Mississippi State Sovereignty Commission was now determined to preserve Jim Crow.

CHAPTER 4

The Pipeline

As the Commission propaganda machine ground out its self-serving distortions, Coleman decided to add to its arsenal. He began setting up a secret investigative unit that would be patterned after the FBI and U.S. military intelligence agencies during wartime, "seeking out intelligence information about the enemy and what the enemy proposed to do." Specifically, Coleman wanted a small team of investigators to infiltrate the NAACP and to keep him apprised of its plans to form new chapters, organize protest demonstration, boycott businesses, and file lawsuits.

The governor began hiring investigators and assigned them to develop a network of paid and unpaid informants to serve as the Commission's "eyes and ears" in communities statewide. The agents found willing collaborators in white civic leaders, businessmen, sheriffs, deputies, judges, and ministers. Determined to stop creeping integration, the informants began calling the Commission office in the New State Capital Building in Jackson, reporting conversations overheard between "Negro agitators," rumors of upcoming protest actions, and the names and descriptions of suspected NAACP leaders in their midst. The Commission agents dubbed this network of neighborhood spies the "pipeline."

—o

Building the white information pipeline was easy compared to the task of recruiting blacks to inform on other blacks. But as one Commission report would conclude, "This problem will never be solved without the help of the Negroes in the state of Mississippi." The agents began quietly soliciting conservative black community leaders to serve as confidential informants, offering payments of $10 to $500 per assignment to keep tabs on suspicious neighbors, or to join the NAACP and send its meeting notes, plans, and member lists to handlers at the Commission.

At first most black informants were small-time operators, but in the spring of 1957, agents began cozying up to Percy Greene, the editor and publisher of the *Jackson Advocate*, the largest circulation black newspaper in the state. The word was that the outspoken, cigar-chomping newspaperman was uneasy with the NAACP's demands for immediate school integration and felt out-of-step with its younger, more opinionated leaders. In addition, Greene needed cash to shore up his financially strapped weekly newspaper and wasn't choosy about his sources of income. The big-talking editor liked to brag that he'd take money from the devil if it meant selling more papers.

After a series of meetings with publicity chief DeCell, Greene made good on his boast and formed a devil's bargain with the Commission. He would publish its propaganda in his newspaper and keep tabs on the NAACP. The Commission would cover his travel expenses to out-of-state meetings and funnel money to him under the guise of subscriptions, advertising, and printing jobs.

Greene hammered the NAACP in his columns and editorials, condemning its "vindictive speeches" against "responsible white people" and began funneling information to the Commission. And he made a handsome side income. In 1958 alone, Greene received $3,200 from the Commission—more than $24,000 in today's money.

—o

Shortly after wooing and winning Greene, the spies scored an even bigger prize. Reverend Henry Harrison Humes—one of the most influential African American ministers in the state—agreed to serve as a confidential informant. Rev. H. H. Humes was the long-time pastor of New Hope Baptist Church in Greenville, editor of the weekly *Delta Leader*, and president of the 387,000-member Baptist State Convention, the largest black Baptist organization in Mississippi. Now he was riding a circuit of black churches across the Mississippi River Delta, building a loyal following through his powerful oratory and moral decrees. Humes had significant influence over ordinary churchgoers, a powerful voice in church affairs, and plenty of contacts within the NAACP.

A conservative black preacher supporting segregation was rare but not completely unheard of in Mississippi at that time. White community leaders often bestowed special status on "Negro preachers" for keeping politics out of the pulpit and their flocks focused on the rewards of the afterlife rather than the shortcomings of the here-and-now. Black ministers who toed the line received contributions to their church funds, special relationships with white community leaders, and even a voice in state affairs. Humes was cut from that cloth.

As an informant, Humes proved himself by providing intelligence on NAACP recruitment in his hometown of Greenville. His first check was for a modest $29.76 for "investigations." A February 11, 1957, memo recommended paying him $150 to spy on other black preachers at an upcoming regional ministerial meeting in Atlanta, because his report "could alert us to local situations." Now the preacher was set to make serious money.

Humes followed up the initial assignments with such detailed information and enticing leads that his handlers steadily upped his pay. Before long, the minister was receiving a $150 monthly salary and additional payments for special assignments. The 55-year-old preacher became the primary source of anti–civil rights intelligence in the Delta, providing advance word on NAACP meetings, warnings of visits from out-of-state leaders, whispers of future actions, and the names and addresses of new members and aspiring leaders. Humes was so thorough that he even hired a stenographer to record NAACP meetings word-for-word. He mailed meticulous reports to the Commission office and frequently drove to Jackson to brief his handlers in person.

—o

Then, in July of 1957, everything changed. Greene and Humes were exposed. The Associated Press broke a story stating that two black leaders were pocketing under-the-table payments from a public agency dedicated to preserving segregation. The proof: state-issued checks made out to Greene and Humes from the Sovereignty Commission. The civil rights community was outraged by the betrayal. NAACP leaders complained that their work to secure equal rights for ordinary people had been jeopardized by a couple of well-heeled Uncle Toms. Grassroots activists grumbled that they were going to jail for the cause while well-to-do community members were on the payroll of the jailers. The leadership of the NAACP fired back at the informants. NAACP Executive Director Roy Wilkins told a packed crowd of 600 people at the Mount Bethel Baptist Church in Gulfport that Greene and Humes were "quick to get their hands in the till."

Humes denied the allegations. Speaking to hundreds of people packed into the pews, he charged that the NAACP had "fallen into bad hands." But Humes' supporters were slow to rally to his defense, and his enemies were quick on the attack. NAACP members circulated a petition calling for his removal as president of the Baptist Convention. A coalition of black preachers issued a statement calling him "unworthy of the fellowship of the ministers of the Protestant denominations in Mississippi."

Deflated by the attacks and fearful of being exposed again by reporters, Humes cut back on his spying and stopped traveling to Jackson to file reports, instead meeting his handlers at secret locations to plead for their support in clearing his name. He became consumed by the vendetta against him and depressed over his fall from grace.

Then, one night while driving home from a friend's house, the minister became violently ill. He made his way to a doctor's office, where he suffered a seizure and died of a heart attack. The next day Humes' Commission contact sent a memo to Governor Coleman saying, "The death of Rev. Humes has cost us one of the most influential Negroes we have had working on our behalf." Later, the agent drove to the minister's house in Greenville and, unbeknownst to the grieving family, slipped into Humes' office "to remove all files dealing with the Sovereignty Commission."

—o

The exposure of the black informants lifted a curtain on the state's secret spy network. Now, NAACP leaders were keenly aware of the dangers posed by those curious men in suits who had been jotting down the tag numbers of cars parked outside their meeting places. Civil rights activists were taking steps to protect their confidential documents and calling out suspected snitches in their meetings. For its part, the Commission quickly replaced Humes with one of his followers and added more informants—white and black—to its intelligence pipelines. As for Greene, he weathered the storm and continued informing and publishing propaganda. The two sides were poised for conflict, and there was more controversy bubbling up from the rich, black Mississippi River Delta.

CHAPTER 5

The Delta Blues

The Mississippi River Delta is a study in contrast. The vast stretches of green and white cotton fields are interspersed with eerie, moss-draped cypress swamps. The white-pillared mansions of the plantation elite stand near the ramshackle huts of the poor dirt farmer. The delta is home to debutante balls and backroom gambling dens, ramshackle houseboats and majestic paddle wheelers. The sweltering, insect-ridden, and amazingly fertile stretch of bottomland forms, in the words of author James C. Cobb, "the most Southern place on earth."

—○

Back in the 1860s, hundreds of thousands of slaves worked the vast cotton fields, afraid to resist or to run for fear of being whipped, beaten, or sold away from their families. Each day, more black men, women, and children were delivered to the plantations by slave brokers, who purchased their human cargo in the bustling markets of New Orleans and Natchez, marching them in groups of about 30 for hundreds of miles to their oppressive new homes. The seemingly endless supply of slave labor and a ravenous demand for cotton fueled a robust economy dominated by wealthy planters, powerful politicians, and influential businessmen.

—○

The legacy of slavery, the grip of widespread rural poverty, and an almost total lack of educational opportunities made it virtually impossible for civil rights workers to organize effectively in the delta prior to the 1950s. The small cotton-processing towns and enclaves along the Mississippi River seemed destined to be racially segregated and brutally oppressive for African Americans for generations to come. But by the late 1950s, in the hardscrabble delta town of Clarksdale, a mild-mannered pharmacist and drugstore owner was beginning to make progress. Aaron Henry, president of the Coahoma County NAACP chapter and executive secretary of the Regional Council of Negro Citizens, was organizing the black community, petitioning the school board to integrate schools, speaking out against the harassment of black voters. Affectionately known to his friends in the black community as "Doc," Henry had even turned his Fourth Street drugstore into a makeshift community center and school to prepare poor dirt famers to vote for the first time.

Henry had grown up in a sharecropping family on the Flowers Brothers Plantation. He escaped poverty by joining the Army and learned his pharmacy craft at Xavier College in New Orleans. After college, he returned home to the delta, drawn by the lure of the land and a determination to end racial prejudice. "You know that old Mississippi River has never had an ounce of racial prejudice," he liked to say. "When it comes to bursting over those levees, it doesn't stop to ask where the colored section is. It just takes all."

The Commission spies initially underestimated Henry's effectiveness, bragging of duping him into divulging valuable information without even knowing it. But over time, Henry's relentless organizing and alliance building forced the spies to enhance their surveillance. In early 1958, Commission agent Zach Van Landingham traveled to Clarksdale to meet with a prominent judge and White Citizens' Council leader to discuss the growing clamor for equality among blacks in Clarksdale. Van Landingham discovered that the leading white citizens had a plan to rid themselves of the pharmacist-turned-crusader. The Council would pressure pharmaceutical wholesalers to stop selling supplies to Henry's drugstore and would press local doctors to refuse to write prescriptions for patients who shopped there. The economic squeeze would bankrupt Henry, forcing him to leave town in search of work. The Council also planned to persuade the superintendent of Coahoma Country Negro School District to fire Henry's wife, Nicole, from her teaching job just to make sure the Henrys had no reason to stay in town. "It is believed that if Henry leaves the area," Van Landingham reported back to his superiors at the Commission, "the NAACP will die."

—o

The Commission surrounded Henry with black informants, who infiltrated his meetings, intercepted his
documents, and even eavesdropped at his church. One
investigative report noted that an informant code-named
J 1 "advised that he had been listening very closely in his
church," and it appeared that NAACP meetings were "not
well attended" and that Henry was not "doing very well
with his drugstore." But Henry kept holding meetings,
signing up members, registering voters, and speaking out
in the press. NAACP membership and black voter registration in the region crept upward.

Then, late in 1958, Henry was elected president of the
Mississippi branch of the NAACP, making him one of the
most important civil rights leaders in the state. Despite
the recognition and the stature, his struggle was really
just beginning. Over time his wife would be fired from her
teaching job, his drugstore would be firebombed, and he
would be arrested and jailed on false charges. As punish-
ment, he would be tied to the back of a garbage truck and
forced to load trash in full view of his neighbors. But the
sight of an unrelenting freedom worker tethered to a trash
truck only enhanced his stature in the black community.

Death of a Dream

Clyde Kennard climbed into his 1958 Mercury station
wagon and drove from the black farming hamlet of
Eatonville to the stately, all-white campus of Mississippi
Southern College. The pristine campus, with its red-brick
walkways, white-columned buildings, and shimmering
lily ponds, seemed a world away from the family poultry farm that he was working for his ailing mother in
Eatonville. The former Army paratrooper and University
of Chicago political science major was headed to the
office of Mississippi Southern President W.D. McCain to
get word on his application to enroll at the college. The
30-year-old Kennard was all too aware that he had stirred
up a hornet's nest by applying to an all-white public college, but he had no idea that he was walking into a set-up
of epic proportions. Commission investigator agent?
Zack Van Landingham was waiting for him in President
McCain's office—as was a formal letter of rejection. The

police were also watching and waiting with dangerous intensions in mind. And Kennard's troubles were just beginning. The Commission role in his undoing would prove that its extraordinary powers were far beyond the point of being "contained."

—o

Clyde Kennard was born on June 12, 1927, and raised among the cotton and corn fields of rural Forrest County, Mississippi. At age 12, his family sent him to live with his sister in Chicago to have a chance to attend decent schools. In 1945 Kennard enlisted in the Army. He graduated from paratrooper school, served as a paratrooper in Korea and Germany, and rose to the rank of sergeant. In 1952, he received an honorable discharge, with the Bronze Star, Korean Service Medal, United Nations Service Medal, and Good Conduct Medal to his credit.

After his discharge, Kennard earned a high-school diploma, began taking college courses, and enrolled full-time at the University of Chicago. He completed two years toward a political science degree. Then he got bad news: His stepfather was dying, and his ailing mother couldn't keep up the farm. In the spring of 1954, at age 28, Kennard left the University of Chicago for the family chicken farm in Mississippi.

Kennard worked diligently to turn the farm into a profitable operation. He got a part-time job at a department store in Hattiesburg to earn extra cash for the family. His dream of a college education was still calling, however, and he began to think about Mississippi Southern College (now the University of Southern Mississippi). The campus was just 15 minutes from his house, it offered night classes, and it would accept transfer credits from the University of Chicago.

—o

Kennard applied for admission in 1956. His application was denied as "incomplete." He reapplied in 1958. It was denied again for alleged "irregularities." Then, in December of 1959, Kennard applied again. This time he explained his decision—and openly mocked the idea of separate but equal schools—in an editorial in the *Hattiesburg American* "Are we to assume that two sets of hospitals are to be built for two groups of doctors? Are we to build two bridges across the same stream to give equal opportunity to two groups of engineers? Are we to have two courts of law so as to give both groups of lawyers the same chance to demonstrate their skills; two legislatures for our politically inclined; and of course two governors?" On integration and racial cooperation, Kennard concluded, "I would rather meet my God with this creed than with any other yet devised by human society."

Suddenly, the Army veteran, college student, and poultry farmer had captured public attention. The national [?] press jumped on the story of a black military veteran seeking to break the color barrier in higher education in

Mississippi. The NAACP offered legal assistance in case Kennard decided to sue the college for discrimination. And the next entry in the Commission secret file read in understated fashion, "The Clyde Kennard problem is no longer simply a local concern."

—o

Agent Van Landingham immediately began working up an investigation, relying on the initial groundwork provided by a confidential investigator code -named T1. The exhaustive probe examined Kennard's childhood in Hattiesburg, his upbringing in Chicago, his years in the military, and his time in college and on the farm. The agents interviewed his friends, teachers, ministers, and business associates and sent a bank examiner to the Citizens' Bank of Hattiesburg to inspect his accounts. The search turned up nothing that could be used to undercut his application. "Persons who know Kennard describe him as intelligent, well educated, quiet spoken, courteous with a desire to better the Negro race," Van Landingham reported.

The investigators were so intent on finding damning information that their reports presented the most mundane facts with sinister implication. The agents noted that as a student Kennard joined the Progressive Citizens' Club and the German Club. Furthermore, "the files of confidential agent T1 reflect that Clyde Kennard has no middle name."

With little to go on, Van Landingham paid a visit to Dudley W. Conner, head of the White Citizens' Council of

Hattiesburg. Without prodding, Connor offered to have his Council henchmen "take care of him." When pressed by the investigator on the meaning behind that menacing statement, Dudley explained "Kennard's car could be hit a train or he could have some accident on the highway and no one would ever know the difference."

As an alternative to the Council's extreme approach, Van Landingham devised a more moderate plan to pressure Kennard to drop his application. As part of the agent's plan, Governor Coleman invited Kennard to a meeting in Jackson and offered to get him into a segregated Negro college or even an integrated university in the North. Short of that, the governor appealed to Kennard to hold off on his application until the controversy over it "cooled down," maybe after the next election.

Van Landingham also organized a committee of influential black educators to lobby Kennard to drop his application. The educators agreed to make the case in exchange for the governor's support for a state-funded Negro Junior College in Hattiesburg. They pleaded with Kennard to take back the application, warning that his attempt to become the first black admitted to an all-white college could lead to trouble, even bloodshed.

Kennard refused to back down. Now, for him, it was a matter of principle.

—o

The fateful meeting between Kennard and Mississippi Southern President McCain was set for Tuesday, September 15, 1959, at 9:30 a.m. The entire meeting lasted just 20 minutes. McCain and Van Landingham implored Kennard to give up, but he politely held his ground. Then Mississippi Southern admissions director Aubrey Lucas was called into the office to hand Kennard the official letter of rejection, which claimed that his University of Chicago transcripts were incomplete and that his physical examination records had been altered, proving that he lacked the moral character to attend the prestigious college.

Kennard left the office and walked slowly back toward his car. In the distance he saw two campus police officers standing next to his station wagon. Constables Charlie Ward and Lee Daniels confronted him, accused him of speeding through the campus, and placed him under arrest for reckless driving. As one of the constables took Kennard into custody, the other opened the station wagon and planted five half-pints of liquor under the front seat. Later that day, Kennard was charged with reckless driving and possession of liquor. At that time Mississippi was a dry state and possessing liquor was technically illegal even though it was sold openly and was widely available.

After learning of the arrest, Van Landingham called the governor's office with the news. He told Coleman's administrative assistant, "It appeared to be a frame up with the planting of evidence in his car."

CHAPTER 7

The Savior of Segregation

Throughout his campaign for governor, Ross Barnett traveled the state stoking the fears of small-town white voters with racially charged stump speeches. His voice moved from soft cadence to rolling thunder as he warned that their "cherished way of life" was being threatened by the "integrationists, agitators, subversives, and race mixers.

"I am a Mississippi segregationist and proud of it," Barnett said to wild cheers, the crowds whooping, stomping their feet and shouting back, "You tell 'em, Ross."

Barnett had lost two previous campaigns for governor but this time had an added advantage. The successful private attorney and former Klansman had been handpicked and endorsed by the White Citizens' Council, which now claimed more than 80,000 members.

On the campaign trail, Barnett zeroed in on the federal government. He knew that the Supreme Court school desegregation ruling was just the beginning of a steady federal assault on segregation. The U.S. Justice Department had formed a special division to make sure the states enforced a growing body of civil rights laws. Congress was considering sweeping new legislation to mandate integration in public buildings, parks, and playgrounds and to ban racial discrimination in the workplace. Furthermore a young, liberal Massachusetts congressman named John F. Kennedy was running for President. For the first time, a viable candidate for the nation's highest office was courting the black vote. Barnett knew change was coming. He also knew that fear of that change was his ticket to power.

Barnett told voters that the national politicians were trampling Mississippi's right to govern itself. His campaign workers even nailed posters to telephone poles in small towns warning that only he could stop "the occupation forces from the N.A.A.C.P. and the specially trained goon squads from the Justice Department."

With his arms waving and voice trembling, he pledged that no public school, park, swimming pool, or restroom would be integrated on his watch. And in the end this fierce segregationist, with a flair for drama that would become his hallmark, summed up his position on integration with one word: "Never!"

Barnett also criticized departing Governor Coleman for failing to use the Commission to neutralize the enemy. The fact that Barnett had no knowledge of the Commission's

secret operations didn't stop him from charging the segregation watchdogs with sleeping on the job.

Since Governor Coleman was ineligible to run for a
consecutive second term under state law, Lieutenant
Governor J. Carroll Gartin opposed Barnett in the
key Democratic primary. Gartin—a moderate on race
in the Coleman tradition—could not rile up as much
segregationist fervor as his demagogic rival. By the
time the critical primary election was held in August of
1959, the Barnett campaign had worked white voters
into a frenzy of fear. Barnett won by a comfortable
margin, and—since the Republican Party had no viable
candidate for the general election—he had a lock on the
governorship. Upon hearing the news of Barnett's victory,
outgoing Governor Coleman said, "May the good Lord
help us for the next four years." With that, Ross Barnett
rode a wave of white fear into the governor's mansion.

The Clandestine War

On a cold, gray day in January of 1960, Ross Barnett
delivered his inaugural address. "You know and I know,"
he reassured his fellow white citizens, "that we will
maintain segregation in Mississippi at all costs." The
small-town boy who dreamed of growing up to become
an important man had realized his greatest ambition.
Barnett would relish the architectural excesses of the governor's mansion (he would install gold-plated faucets in
the bathrooms) and the State Capital Building, with its 16
different kinds of marble and its bronze statue of former
Governor and U.S. Senator Theodore Bilbo, an openly
racist and corrupt powermonger who proudly referred
to himself as "The Man." Now Ross Barnett was the new
man—and his rise to power proved that classic race bait-
ing could still win elections in the Magnolia State.

  After settling into his office, Barnett received status
reports, investigative memos, and personal briefings on

the Commission and attended regular meetings of its governing board. The new governor expected the spies to wage a real clandestine war against the civil rights movement. But how? He had no set of directions for building a secret police force and no owner's manual for running a covert spy network. He was just the son of a Civil War veteran from the farming hamlet of Standing Pine, who grew up with an obsessive dream of wearing fine suits, making important speeches, and standing in the limelight. He had worked his way through law school, built a successful law practice, and become president of the Mississippi Bar Association, finally rising to power as a classic white supremacist, who once proclaimed, "God is the ultimate segregationist. He made the white man white and the Negro black and never intended them to mix."

But behind his back, Barnett was not always given the respect he longed for. He was often mocked as a chronic bumbler, and his actions frequently added to the snickers. Speaking at a breakfast meeting with Jewish community leaders at a local synagogue, he thanked the members of B'nai Brith for joining him in "fine Christian fellowship." He once injured himself on an airport tarmac by stepping into the whirling propeller blade of his own campaign airplane. He would become the only governor to name two Miss Americas honorary colonels in the Mississippi National Guard.

Barnett's antics hid his raw intelligence, ambition, and

persistence in his quest for power. He knew how to charm his friends and disarm his enemies with his courtly demeanor, down-home storytelling, quick wit, and low-brow humor. He also knew how power worked and applied that knowledge to transforming the Commission.

With the support of the state legislature, he doubled the Commission budget and increased its staff. He fired an investigator who had chafed at his campaign claim of Commission foot-dragging, sending a clear message that the "moderate" course of the Coleman years was over. Barnett also stacked the Commission board with political allies who shared his views on race. Through his first year in office, Barnett and his allies took several steps to transform the agency into a more effective weapon of information war.

—o

Step 1: Enlist Powerful Allies

In the most controversial move, Barnett pressed state officials to allow the Commission to funnel taxpayer dollars directly into the coffers of the White Citizens' Council. The Commission funding would begin at $5,000 a month for a speakers' program and total more than $200,000 over a number of years—more than $1.2 million in today's currency. And with the added legitimacy of public funding, the Council would position itself as a quasi-official arm of state government, pushing its way into other state agencies, acquiring confidential government information, collaborating with law enforcement, and demanding more and more power.

Step 2: Know Your Enemies

The Commission added a new director of investigations and a number of new agents to its roster, while increasing its use of private detective agencies and "special" free-lance operatives. The typical investigator was a former FBI agent or state police investigator with surveillance experience and a commitment to segregation. Under Barnett, the agents' investigative tactics became more aggressive and their reports increasingly mean-spirited, reflecting their personal opposition to integration and their disdain for their adversaries.

Step 3: Dehumanize the Opposition

The revitalized team immediately launched an extensive "subversive hunt," investigating private citizens for criticizing state officials, belonging to liberal organiza-tions, or supporting unpopular causes. A report issued in March 1961 notes that investigations were being launched against people who were merely speaking out, people whose "utterances or actions indicate they should be watched with suspicion of future racial attitudes."

The investigative files increasingly referred to the op-position as "agitators, subversives, beatniks, do-gooders,

and Communists." The Communist tag was the most
potent weapon even though it was being applied several
years after the fall from grace of U.S. Senator Joseph
McCarthy of Wisconsin, whose finger-pointing ruined
reputations, wrecked careers, and led to his expulsion
from the Senate. In Mississippi, a person accused of being
a Communist was pre-judged a supporter of the Soviet
Union, at a time when that totalitarian nation was align-
ing its allies against the United States.

Step 4: Control the Media

Barnett named his former campaign publicist Earle
Johnston as the Commission's public relations director.
Johnston was a former newspaper reporter, editor, and
publisher with solid ties to journalists in the Mississippi
press corps. He also knew how the national media
worked and had connections at national news services
and TV networks. Johnston was the perfect choice to
work both sides of the story. He would adeptly paint the
Commission as a benign public relations operation simply
representing the positive side of race relations in the
state. Behind the scenes, he would fine-tune the propaganda bible, emphasizing the soft sell of segregation.
"This is a selling job and it cannot be done by waving red
flags or using emotional approaches," he advised. "Facts,
situations, and an appeal for understanding will be more
effective in gaining support for the south."

Johnston expanded the propaganda package to include carefully crafted speeches, articles by black segregationists, and a 27-minute film entitled "The Message of Mississippi," which "showed in scenes and interviews the racial harmony that exists among the vast majorities of each race."

Step 5: Set Moral Standards

The revitalized team launched a campaign to remove "subversive" books from the shelves of schools and public libraries. The Commission's education and information unit listed books that contained sections on desegregation or labor organizations as unacceptable and suggested replacing them with books that advocated segregation and white supremacy. It also presented programs at dozens of colleges and high schools detailing the evils of Communism and loaned books, films, and speeches on racial separation and white supremacy to young readers.

Never, Never Land

The cry of "Never" from die-hard segregationists in
Mississippi infuriated advocates for integration, who
responded by dubbing the state "Never, Never Land."
The tag fit. The deep racial divide, widespread poverty,
and isolation kept Mississippi in a sort of social time
warp. Mississippi had no major cosmopolitan center
like Atlanta, New Orleans, or Memphis, where large
newspapers carried competing points of view and major
universities debated new ideas. When a commercial
airliner circled to land at the Jackson airport, pilots
playfully instructed passengers to fasten their seatbelts
and set their watches back 50 years.

The fundamentals of segregation only began to
describe the complicated world that Mississippians—
approximately 55 percent white and 45 percent black—
had to navigate at the time. A black woman was allowed
to shop in a white-owned department store but could not

try on clothes because the dressing rooms were reserved for "whites only." A black child could be admitted into a public hospital but could not play with white children in the waiting area of the pediatrics ward. Black men and women were expected to respect white people at all times but were not to be addressed as Mr., Mrs., or Miss by whites. Both whites and blacks loved to attend the big event of the year: the Mississippi State Fair. It lasted for two weeks each summer—one week for white patrons and one week for "colored" patrons. These complex lines had to be understood and adhered to or very carefully sidestepped.

As the civil rights crusaders pressed for change, the white power structure pulled back hard. And with Barnett in the governor's office, the state moved toward an even harsher form of white resistance.

—○

The harsher tactics also played a role in the continuing saga of Clyde Kennard, the military veteran who had been denied admission to all-white Mississippi Southern College. Kennard, who had been framed by the police for possession of liquor, soon found himself in another run-in with the law. This chapter in the saga began when the Forest County Cooperative warehouse was burglarized. The day before, 19-year-old Johnny Lee Roberts had been loading trucks and had purposely left a door to the warehouse unlocked. The next morning, Roberts

reentered the building and stole five bags of chicken
feed worth $25. In short order, Roberts was arrested
and grilled by police. Under pressure to confess, Roberts
claimed that his friend, Clyde Kennard, had put him up
to it. Police searched Kennard's farm and came back with
a couple of empty feed bags. Kennard was charged as an
accomplice to burglary—a felony. At trial Roberts made a
meandering, hard-to-follow account of the robbery that
confused even the district attorney. Still, it took an all-
white jury only 10 minutes to hand down guilty verdicts.
Roberts got a suspended sentence and was rehired by the
co-op. Kennard, by contrast, was sentenced to the maximum penalty—seven years at hard labor at the notorious
Mississippi State Penitentiary at Parchman. How bad was
Parchman? The prison farm, constructed after the Civil
War as a direct response to the abolition of slavery, was
originally designed to instill young, wayward black men
with discipline that could no longer be administered by
the whips of slave owners.

At the maximum security penitentiary, Kennard
worked from sun up to sundown on the prison cotton
farm. He urged his mother not to visit—"just make believe
I'm back in the Army." He spent Sundays writing letters
for illiterate prisoners. The NAACP worked without
success to overturn his conviction but managed to
publicize his plight. Then, after two years of hard time,
Kennard doubled over with stomach pain. He was rushed

to the hospital and diagnosed with intestinal cancer. Doctors operated immediately, but the cancer had spread throughout his body. The doctors recommended that Kennard be released, given "the extremely poor prognosis in this rather young patient." But Governor Barnett, determined to send a message to any future would-be integrationists, refused to grant clemency. Barnett ordered that the dying man be returned to prison, where he was sent back into the cotton fields.

With Kennard's condition worsening, an outcry built up in the northern black press. Black comedian Dick Gregory, who had gained celebrity status entertaining white and black nightclub audiences and appearing on national TV, charged that the military veteran, college student, and farmer had been framed, railroaded into prison, abused, neglected, and left for dead.

Overflowing the Jails

— May 24, 1961 —

I'm taking a ride on the Greyhound bus line
I'm taking a ride to Jackson this time
Hallelujah I'm a traveling
Halleluiah, ain't it fine
Hallelujah I'm a traveling
Down freedom's main line

In May of 1961, a red, silver, and white double-decked bus raced down Highway 80 in Alabama. The bus was escorted by 16 state police cars and shadowed by L-19 reconnaissance aircraft and helicopters. Onboard were 12 civil rights activists, 10 news reporters, and 8 National Guardsmen with grim faces and bayonet-tipped rifles. The odd assortment of passengers fell silent at the sight of the border-side sign: "Welcome to the Magnolia State." As the bus crossed the state line, one of the riders broke the tension with the quip: "We just got into a foreign country!"

As the caravan raced forward, Mississippi National Guardsmen fanned out along a wooded stretch of the route, alerted to a tip that Klansmen planned to dynamite the bus shortly after it crossed the state line. Driving through stop signs and traffic lights, the convoy finally reached the city limits of Jackson and rolled to its destination: the interstate bus terminal. The time had come for the long-awaited showdown between the young activists and the Jackson City Police.

The protesters bounded off the bus and walked quickly toward the terminal. The black riders headed to the "whites only" waiting room, and the one white rider headed to the room marked "Negros only." Jackson police issued two warnings and began making arrests. The police ran the protestors through a gauntlet of officers to waiting paddy wagons and shuttled them off to the local lock-up. The first Freedom Ride to Mississippi of the summer of 1961 had been carried out in perfect choreography. Federal officials, state officials, Freedom Riders, and police breathed a sigh of relief. Violence had been avoided. At that time, none of them knew that waves of additional buses with hundreds of new riders would soon be en route to Jackson to repeat the process again, and again, and again.

—o

Three weeks earlier, Freedom Riders had boarded busses in Washington, D.C., determined to expose segregated waiting rooms, rest rooms, and water fountains
in bus stations and train depots in the South. The U.S.
Supreme Court had barred segregation in interstate
travel in 1960, but the ruling was being ignored south
of the Mason-Dixon line. As the Freedom Riders moved
into the Deep South, angry white mobs were waiting
with insults, threats, bottles, and rocks. Then, outside
Anniston, Alabama, an angry mob of 200 people stoned
a bus, slashed its tires, and hit it with a firebomb. In
Birmingham, Alabama, a mob overturned a bus and beat
the fleeing riders with baseball bats and chains.

In light of the violence, protest organizers with the
Congress of Racial Equality (CORE) prepared to call a
halt to the rides. Then, U.S. Attorney General Robert
Kennedy brokered a deal with officials in Alabama and
Mississippi to prevent future violence should the rides
continue on to Jackson. The state officials promised to
provide state police and guard protection for the riders
if local police could arrest protesters at the bus termi-
nals for breach of peace. That's when a group of young
activists from the newly formed Student Non-violent
Coordinating Committee (SNCC, pronounced Snick)
volunteered to make the trip to Jackson., Led by seemingly fearless young activists such as Diane Nash, the
Freedom Riders set out. The eyes of the nation and the

world—stunned by the news accounts of the Alabama attacks and shocked that young students would put their lives on the line—were focused on the drama. All eyes were on Mississippi.

—○

Governor Barnett, the Mississippi Highway Patrol, the Jackson City Police, and the Sovereignty Commission were waiting with a plan. From their point of view, the best course was to avert violence—along with the negative, worldwide press coverage it would spawn. The police planned to break up white crowds before they became mobs and to arrest protesters without brutality and charge them with simple breach of peace. In all likelihood, the local courts would issue suspended sentences and modest fines, and the freed students would return home with the Northern reporters close behind.

Behind the scenes, the Commission agents would create files on the Freedom Riders, including their names, addresses, organizational ties, and mug shots. The investigators would run background checks in the riders' home states in search of information that could be used to discredit the movement as "subversive and Communist." The files would be shared with law enforcement agencies in other Southern states and used to identify repeat offenders. If all went according to plan, the Commission propaganda machine would churn out the story that Mississippi whites had not resorted to violence, and

Mississippi blacks had not joined the protests, proving
that segregation was key to peaceful race relations.

—o

Not surprisingly, all did not go according to their plan.
Two weeks into the saga, the first wave of riders was
taken to court for an arraignment hearing. Judge James
Spencer found the students guilty and issued $200 fines
and 60-day suspended sentences. At that point, the young
and idealistic riders rewrote the script. Determined to
keep the spotlight on segregation by "filling the jails to
overflowing," the riders refused to admit their guilt or
pay their fines. The white riders were returned to the
relatively modern Jackson City Jail and black prisoners to
the grim Hinds County Jail. And with dozens of students
boarding Jackson-bound busses and trains, the goal of
filling the jails looked attainable.

A month into the stalemate, the state introduced its
response to jail overcrowding. Groups of prisoners were
herded from their cells and loaded on gray vans with
metal seats and barred windows. The vans drove out of
town and into the country. The landscape moved from
green hills to vast, flat stretches of green and white cotton
fields and creepy cypress swamps. Some 140 miles into
the trip, the riders looked through the barred windows
and glimpsed a frightening scene. Prison inmates in
black-and-white-striped garb chopped cotton in the fields
under the gaze of guards on horseback with rifles draped

over their arms. In the distance stood the barbed-wire fences and looming guard towers of the maximum security penitentiary at Parchman. The van crawled through the gate and into the inner core of the prison, stopping at the maximum security unit that housed death row inmates, solitary confinement cells, and the electric chair.

The students were marched down grim walkways to even darker cell blocks. The men were led to cells adjacent to other inmates. The women were taken to an isolated unit. All were issued prison clothes, a Bible, an aluminum cup, and a toothbrush. For the first two days, the inmates lived in fear of being beaten by the guards—or "screws"—until it became clear that their national media status was assuring them hands-off treatment. Confined to the maximum-security unit day and night with only their Bibles to read, the riders passed the time singing freedom songs. The warden and guards—concerned that the soulful melodies and defiant lyrics could inspire other inmates to join in—repeatedly ordered the singers to stop. When the singing continued, the guards began taking away items of clothing, toothbrushes, and mattresses.

CORE organizer James Farmer recalled one singer's response: "He said: 'Come take my mattress. I'll keep my soul.' And everybody started singing, 'Ain't gunna let no body turn me 'round, turn me 'round, turn me 'round.'"

One night the guards introduced a new tactic by removing screens from cell-block windows. Swarms of mosquitoes flowed into the cells. And worse was on the way: "A guard came in and said 'Look at all them bugs. We're gunna have to spray,'" recalled Freedom Rider David Frankhauser. "Shortly thereafter, we heard what sounded like a large diesel truck pull up outside the cell block. And what looked like a fire hose was passed in through one of the high windows. As the engine fired up outside, we were hit with a powerful spray of DDT. Being trapped in our cells, with no protection, our bodies, and every inch of our cells, were drenched with the eye-stinging, skin-burning insecticide."

Five weeks into the summer stalemate, more than 150 Freedom Riders had been arrested and convicted and waves of additional buses were en route to Jackson. Northern newspaper accounts of alleged abuses at Parchman prompted demands that independent delegations be allowed in to inspect conditions and interview the prisoners. Mississippi officials needed a bold new story to change the headlines.

—o

Commission Publicity Director Erle (spelled Earle on p. 40) Johnston had headed North in an effort to persuade skeptical audiences that all was returning to normal in Jackson. In late June, he told a gathering at the Rotary Club in Pocatello, Idaho, that the "self-styled" Freedom Riders had "failed" to reveal a dark side to Southern segregation. To the contrary, Johnston claimed that riders had "brought many representatives of the news media into Mississippi who were able to learn firsthand how the two races work and live in harmony." Looking his audience in the eye, the public relations man claimed that the riders had inadvertently "done the state a service."

At about that time, Commission investigator Andy Hopkins began corresponding with R. J. Strictland, the chief investigator of the Florida Legislative Investigative Committee. The two were members of a coalition of Southern law enforcement investigators who shared information and tactics for fighting "subversion." Strictland supplied Hopkins—a graduate of the FBI training academy who had worked as an assistant to FBI Director J. Edger Hoover—with a four-page document entitled "Fair Play for Cuba." It contained the names of 202 people who had allegedly flown to Havana, Cuba, four months earlier. Two names on the list—compiled from flight manifests at Miami International Airport— were those of Freedom Riders arrested in Jackson. Was their visit to Cuba—an island nation off the coast of Florida and a Communist ally of the Soviet Union— proof of a link between the civil rights movement and international Communism? Was this the bombshell the state needed to change the headlines?

On June 29, Brigadier General T. B. Birdsong— director of public safety and founder of the Mississippi Highway Patrol—called a press conference to expose the Communist connection. Birdsong promised the assembled journalists that he would remove any guesswork from their reporting by disclosing conclusive proof of a major Communist role in the planning and execution of the Freedom Rides.

He revealed that unnamed "sources" had provided unnamed state investigators with a verified list of 202 names of students who had attended a "Fair Play for Cuba" seminar in Havana the previous February. Birdsong named Kathleen Pleune of Chicago and David Wahlstorm of Madison, Wisconsin, as participants of the Cuban seminar. Both had been arrested as Freedom Riders in Jackson.

"They're pawns in the hands of the Communists," Birdsong charged. He then went on to make a series of allegations that went far beyond the known facts. He claimed that the students attended an intensive workshop on civil disobedience tactics in Cuba conducted by nine agents of the Soviet Union. He stated that the workshop had provided detailed instruction on carrying out "sit-ins and walk-ins and freedom rides"—and that the Russian instructors had "inspired and directed" the entire Freedom Ride movement.

CORE immediately branded the allegations as ridiculous, characterizing the press conference as an unfounded "smear tactic." An attorney for one of the students telegraphed Birdsong with a demand for proof that Soviet agents led a workshop on freedom riding during the Cuban trip. Birdsong backed off the claim. The subsequent reporting made the story relatively clear: the students had gone to Cuba with a leftist group seeking to improve Cuban-American relations, but there were no civil disobedience training sessions led by mysterious Soviet agents and there was no tactical advice on freedom riding. The state's bid to regain the propaganda edge fizzled as the Northern press lost interest. And more Freedom Riders kept coming.

Just a week later an even more insidious piece of propaganda hit the newsstands in Mississippi. This one came from black newsman and Commission collaborator Percy Greene. Greene's *Jackson Advocate* ran an eight-column headline above his feature story daring Reverend Martin Luther King to join a Freedom Ride to Jackson and to get arrested and face the potentially deadly conse-quences at Parchman. On July 6, 1961, the inflammatory article was gleefully covered by the segregationist *Jackson Daily News*, which characterized Dr. King not joining the Freedom Rides as "caddillacking around the country making speeches and taking bows."

—o

Despite the public relations diatribes, the Freedom Riders continued to arrive at the depots, the police continued to make arrests, the judges continued to issue fines, and the guards kept ordering prisoners to stop singing. The scorecard of arrests and convictions that ran regularly in the *Jackson Daily News* was no longer a power statement of the state's ability to punish the "invaders." Now it was a reminder of the persistence of the protestors and the outside media attention it spawned.

As events unfolded in Jackson, quiet but persistent power was being applied to the situation by Washington. U.S. Attorney General Robert Kennedy pushed the Interstate Commerce Commission to issue a regulation specifically barring interstate bus and rail companies from allowing segregation at rail and bus depots. As of September 1, 1961, the "whites only" and "Negros only" signs at bus and rail depots gradually began to come down. The Freedom Riders had won a major victory although it would take more time to fully enforce the anti-segregation law.

When it was all over, 328 riders had been arrested and jailed in Mississippi, their mug shots preserved to this day in the files of the Commission. The mug shots of young faces—innocence mixed with fear mixed with defiance—seem frozen in time, testifying to a life-and-death struggle.

—o

After the riders returned to their colleges in the North, it was left to local civil rights activists to contest the bus and rail stations that remained segregated. With the glare of the media gone, the local activists faced harsh and often degrading opposition.

Fanny Lou Hamer, Annelle Ponder, and June Johnson had been working on a voter registration drive in Greenwood, Mississippi, when they were recruited to take part in a workshop on Freedom Rider tactics in Charleston, South Carolina. On their way home from the workshop, their Greyhound bus stopped at a terminal café in Winona, Mississippi. The café had a prominent "whites only" sign on its glass door. The newly trained African American Freedom Riders walked through the door, sat at the counter, and ordered Cokes and bags of peanuts. The restaurant manager told them that Negros could only be served through the rear window and asked them to leave. When they refused, he called the sheriff's office. The three were arrested and taken to the county jail, where they were denied lawyers and placed in separate cells. Then, a black female trustee—an inmate assigned to assist the prison staff—came to Hamer's cell and escorted her to a booking room, where the jailer was waiting with a thick, three-inch wide, leather belt with a handle at one end. The jailer ordered Hamer to bend over a table and pull down her skirt. Then he handed the belt to the trustee. A beating ensued. In short order, Hamer and the other women were found guilty of breach of peace, fined $100, and released.

The NAACP reported the beatings to the U.S. Department of Justice in Washington, D.C. A week later, Justice Department civil rights attorney St. John Barrett

interviewed the women, extracted the details of their
ordeal, and ordered the crime lab to photograph their
still visible wounds. Barrett also traveled to Mississippi
with a tape recorder to interview the jail trustee who had
administered the beating. In his personal memoir, Barrett
recalled the interview:

> *"What were you in jail for?"*
> *"Waiting trial on grand larceny."*
> *"Were you a trusty?"*
> *"Yes, sir."*
> *"What does that mean?"*
> *"That means they trusted me. They would let
> me out of my cell to do the jobs around the jail,
> like mopping the floors, peeling potatoes, wash-
> ing dishes, taking meals to the cells—stuff like
> that."*
> *"Did the jaizwhy they trusted me."*
> *"Did you ever use the strap?"*
> *"Yes sir. He had me use it on the prisoners
> who broke the rules. But I only used it when he
> ordered me to and only for the number of pops
> he ordered."*
> *"When the two women were brought to the
> jail, were you in your cell?"*
> *"No sir. I was mopping the floor."*
> *"Tell me what happened."*

"Well, the police and the jailer put the women in separate cells in the women's section. They didn't book or fingerprint them. The police talked for a while and then the jailer told me to get the heavier woman out of her cell and bring her to the booking room. When I brought her, he told her to take her skirt down and lay on a table on her stomach. She didn't say anything and did like he said. The jailer handed me the strap and told me to give her a few good licks. I gave her a few and he told me to hit her harder and don't stop until he told me to. I kept on going until I saw she was bleeding. I looked at the jailer and he said O.K."

CHAPTER 11

The Battle for Ole Miss

Clyde Kennard had been denied a college education and railroaded into prison, but the dream of breaking the color barrier in higher education in Mississippi lived on. The next attempt came from James Howard Meredith, a Mississippi native, Air Force veteran, and Jackson State College student. Meredith was also a very private person and an intense proponent of racial equality. He was a man with a mission.

Meredith seemed destined to challenge the racial status quo of his native state from as far back as his child-hood in poverty-racked Attala County. His father, "Cap," was a former slave who worked tirelessly to acquire his own land and register to vote. Cap built a fence around his family farm to keep trouble out and taught his son "J. H." to never abide by the custom of entering a white person's house only through the back door.

In the Air Force, J. H. was stationed in Japan, where

he was deeply moved by the acceptance of blacks by the Japanese people. Meredith came home with a strong desire to help his own country become more tolerant. Encouraged by the election of President Kennedy and the integration of several segregated Southern colleges and universities, he began to envision himself breaking the color barrier in Mississippi.

An outstanding student at all-black Jackson State, Meredith applied to transfer to the prestigious University of Mississippi—one of the state's most prominent symbols of white privilege and power. Located in the quaint town of Oxford and steeped in the traditions of the Old South, Ole Miss was the school of choice for the children of Mississippi's white elite. On February 4, 1961, Meredith received a telegram from the Ole Miss admissions officer denying his application. Three days later the Ole Miss Board of Trustees voted to revise the admission rules, giving the school even more leeway to deny him—or any applicant—from entering. The NAACP filed a lawsuit on Meredith's behalf, claiming that he had been denied admission because of his race. The state courts backed the trustees with the dubious ruling that there was no official policy of segregation at Ole Miss even if no black student had ever been enrolled there.

As the case moved through the courts, the Commission sent investigators Andy Hopkins and Virgil Downing to Attala County to prepare a report on Meredith's relationship with his parents. Arriving in the hard-scrabble farming community, the agents stopped at the county courthouse to pore through public records and paid visits to county officials and local police to dig for information. The investigation turned up nothing that would sink Meredith's application. The records showed James Meredith had purchased 84 acres from his father in 1960 and secured license plates for a 1959 Volkswagen and 1952 Cadillac. Sheriff W. T. Wasson told the agents "that he had known Cap Meredith for 20 years and that he knew him to be a good colored person." The black Superintendent of Coahoma County Separate School District, J. T. Coleman, told investigators that James Meredith's mother, Roxie, worked for $14 a week as a cook in the Tipton Street School. Unsolicited, Coleman threatened to fire Roxie if she ever publicly supported her son's aspiration to attend Ole Miss. "Mr. Coleman also stated that should the schools in Mississippi ever be inte-grated, the schools would be ruined," Downing reported, "and that he would do everything he possible could to keep the schools segregated."

The agents concluded that Cap and Roxie Meredith were determined to maintain a low profile, hoping their neighbors would not link them to the man behind the Ole Miss controversy, which had become front-page news even in rural backwaters like Attala County. The agents also knew how to let the entire county know that the "integration agitator" at Ole Miss had roots in their community. Cap and Roxie's low profile was shattered when the agents' investigative report was leaked to the Jackson *Clarion Ledger*. On June 16, 1961, the paper ran a local story headlined "Meredith Drives Cadillac and Compact to Visit Pop." But the spies' small-town maneuverings would soon be eclipsed by stunning national news.

—o

June 25, 1962, was James Meredith's 29th birthday. It was also the day a federal appeals court sent shivers down the spine of the entire white power structure in Mississippi. The Fifth Circuit Court of Appeals overturned the state court ruling, finding that Meredith had been denied entry solely because of his race, victimized by "a carefully calculated campaign of delay, harassment, and masterful inactivity." The U.S. Supreme Court upheld the ruling, setting the stage for a dramatic showdown between Governor Barnett and President Kennedy aided by his brother, Attorney General Robert Kennedy. The clock was ticking. The start of the fall semester was just a few months away.

In July, the Sovereignty Commission rushed Hopkins and Downing back to Attala County in a desperate effort to unearth any damaging information on the Merediths. The investigations again proved fruitless.

As fall approached, Commission Public Relations Director Erle Johnston rushed an order to the printer for more than one million postcards with a pre-printed message expressing resentment at the "unnatural warfare being waged against the sovereign state of Mississippi." The cards—to be signed by white voters throughout the South—were pre-addressed to President Kennedy, White House, Washington, D.C.

On the evening of September 13, Barnett went on statewide television and declared the stand-off "our greatest crisis since the War Between the States," pledging to resist "the evil and illegal forces of tyranny." Repeating his promise that "no school will be integrated while I am your governor," Barnett asked for the resignation of any state official unwilling to "suffer imprisonment for this righteous cause."

On the afternoon of September 20, Barnett, in the first of several dramatic face-to-face confrontations with the federal marshals escorting Meredith, literally stood in the schoolhouse door to stop the enrollment. In a boardroom on the Ole Miss campus, Barnett read a statement denying the application, and the marshals and Meredith walked away to try again another day. In a similar confrontation on September 25, Barnett pulled out his trademark humor to endear himself to his supporters and frustrate his foes. Surrounded by his white supporters as a phalanx of white federal marshals led Meredith into the room, Barnett looked into the sea of white faces and asked: "Which one of you is Mr.

Meredith?" The federal agents scowled, Meredith smiled, and the onlookers howled.

—○

As events continued to unfold, Barnett was buying time by carrying on secret phone conversations with President Kennedy and Attorney General Kennedy, who were now committed to enforcing the court order despite the probable loss of support from powerful Southerners in Congress. The governor tried unsuccessfully to convince the Kennedy brothers to postpone the enrollment indefinitely, warning that bloody riots would shake the campus if a black student was allowed to enroll.

Then, the secret phone negotiations took a bizarre twist. Faced with a federal contempt-of-court charge, a $10,000-per-day fine, and possible jail time, the savior of segregation began to cave to the pressure of possible financial ruin and imprisonment. His hundreds of thousands of white supporters would have been horrified to learn that the chief executive of their "sovereign" state was secretly working with the "forces of tyranny" to assure a black man's peaceful enrollment at Ole Miss. The enemies of segregation were closing in, and Barnett was negotiating the terms of surrender.

The role of the Commission in this affair took a bizarre turn, too. Barnett, needing a point man for the delicate negotiations with the Kennedys, turned to his close friend and confidant Tom Watkins, a successful private attorney and member of the governing board of the Sovereignty Commission. Manning the phone line to Washington, Watkins became the key conduit between Barnett and the Attorney General and the President.

With all sides grappling for a solution, Watkins proposed a series of schemes designed to get Meredith safely ensconced at Ole Miss and allow Barnett to save face. Watkins warned that "if there is to be any school integration in Mississippi, it would have to be done forcefully." In one carefully orchestrated scheme, a federal marshal was to shove Barnett aside and move past him to register the student. Feigning shock, Barnett would save face by condemning the use of federal force against a sitting governor. The stage was set, the actors had their roles, and the curtain was rising when the scene abruptly changed: Barnett's plane was grounded by bad weather in Jackson, leaving Lieutenant Governor Paul Johnson to take his place in Oxford. Unfortunately, no one shared the script with Johnson, who refused to stand aside and pushed back hard against the dumbfounded marshal. The defiant act ingratiated Johnson with the white masses and proved invaluable to his future political career.

Another plan called for the governor and his supporters to make a historic last stand at a gate to Ole Miss, face-to-face with 30 armed federal marshals acting as a shield for Meredith. The lead marshal would pull his gun and point it at Barnett, who would only then call upon his supporters to stand down to avoid bloodshed. When Robert Kennedy repeated the scheme back to Barnett and Watkins over the phone, the governor demurred. He would only sound the retreat if all 30 marshals pulled their weapons and threatened to fire.

"I was under the impression that they were all going to pull their guns," Barnett told an exasperated Robert Kennedy. "If one pulls his gun and we all turn, it would be very embarrassing."

On Saturday, September 29, President Kennedy himself called Barnett to offer a new plan. It called for the governor to rally his forces at the Oxford campus while federal marshals quietly registered Meredith at a state college board office in Jackson. The date was set for Monday, October 1. Barnett could save face by accusing the Kennedys of registering the black student behind his back. Barnett and Watkins agreed to the plan and promised to use the Mississippi Highway Patrol and Mississippi National Guard to maintain calm at Ole Miss.

—o

It turns out that both the Kennedy brothers and Barnett were football fans and, in the parlance of the game, their plan resembled a "hidden ball trick," in which a running back pretends to have the ball while the actual ball carrier, unnoticed, carries it downfield.

So there was some irony that the big football game between Ole Miss and Kentucky was scheduled for Jackson's

Memorial Stadium that very night. At game time, more than 46,000 fans packed the stands, where the Meredith showdown was generating more buzz than the game itself. As Barnett walked to the governor's box, the crowd began waving Confederate flags, chanting "We want Ross. We want Ross." Barnett, the consummate political showman, couldn't resist the adoration. Despite his promise to the Kennedys to maintain calm, he chose to play the hero one more time. At halftime he walked to midfield, stood at a microphone, clinched his fist, waved his arms, and shouted "I love Mississippi, I love her people. I love our customs." The crowd went into a frenzy.

Old Miss student Gerald Blessy recalled the scene years later. "I looked back at the crowd and saw anger in the faces of the people right next to me and it sort of flashed through my mind that those rebel flags looked liked swastikas. These were just ordinary school kids who were being whipped into a fever pitch of emotion by their own leaders. It was just like the Nazis had done."

Commission Public Relations Chief Erle spelling? Johnston had a different recollection of Barnett's speech. "As he stood there, smiling, acknowledging the cheers of the multitude, he was more than a governor of Mississippi. He was a symbol of the South, with the red blood of his Confederate soldier father running through his veins."

After the game, hundreds of students began driving to Oxford, spoiling for a fight.

And Barnett called Washington and left a message for Robert Kennedy: The deal to enroll Meredith was off. In the game to come, there would be no hidden ball trick.

—o

The next morning, Sunday, September 30, an infuriated Attorney General called Barnett with a threat. The President was prepared to go on national television that night to tell the American people that "you had an agreement to permit Meredith to go to Jackson to register, and your lawyer, Mr. Watkins, said this was satisfactory." Barnett's blood ran cold. This would mean that the entire nation—even more important, the entire white power structure of the state of Mississippi —would know that the ardent segregationist and former Klansman had sold out the cause. The official transcript of the phone conversation reads:

> **RB [Ross Barnett]**: *That won't do at all.*
>
> **RFK [Robert Kennedy]**: *You broke your word to him.*
>
> **RB**: *You don't mean the President is going to say that tonight?*
>
> **RFK**: *Of course he is; you broke your word; now you suggest we send in troops, fighting their way through a barricade. You gave your word. Mr. Watkins gave him his word. You didn't keep it.*
>
> **RB**: *Don't say that. Please don't mention it.*

The Attorney General then instructed Barnett and Watkins to prepare a statement to be read by the governor on statewide TV that night, consenting to the enrollment and calling for calm at Ole Miss. Barnett and Watkins wrote a script and later that day reviewed it with Robert Kennedy. The pillar of segregated education in Mississippi fell to earth with these words by Ross Barnett: "My heart says never but my good judgment abhors the bloodshed that would follow.... We must at all odds preserve the peace and avoid bloodshed."

—o

Despite the capitulation, President Kennedy had given up on Barnett. The President decided to take charge. Forget the hidden ball trick. The Kennedys were running through Barnett's front line. The President placed the Mississippi National Guard under his authority and alerted the U.S. Army base at Memphis to prepare for possible deployment to Oxford. As those events unfolded, student mobs began roaming the campus, shouting racial slurs, and hurling rocks and bricks. Hundreds of armed men—including Klansman from across the South and white militias from as far away as California—began arriving in Oxford, ready to take on the federal forces. At about 5:30 p.m., Meredith was escorted to Baxter dormitory by dozens of U.S. marshals wearing gas masks, vests, and helmets and equipped with tear-gas launchers, batons, and sidearms. Within an hour, Ole Miss erupted into a full-scale riot. For hours, clouds of tear gas rode the breeze and the sound of gunshots crackled in the night. Mississippi National Guard troops arrived at about 11 p.m., and Army units showed up at 2 a.m. By the end of the long night, more than 20,000 troops had descended on the campus, seizing control, restoring order, and arresting more than 200 people. Two people were dead, and more than 150 federal agents injured—more than 20 by gunfire. On Monday, October 1, 1962, James H. Meredith attended his first class. The subject was American history.

—o

In a telling footnote, six weeks later Commission investigator Tom Scarborough went to Attala County to continue the investigation into Meredith's parents. Scarborough reported that Cap and Roxie had refused an appeal from Sheriff Wasson to go with him to Jackson to persuade their son to drop out of Ole Miss or—short of that—speak out against his enrollment in the newspapers. The elder Merediths wanted nothing to do with the controversy, insisting that James rarely visited them and never discussed his role at Ole Miss.

Still the agent couldn't resist reporting his personal conclusion: "It is my opinion that both mama and papa Meredith are not opposed to what their now-famous son had done and is doing. To the contrary they are proud of what James Meredith has done by entering the University

of Mississippi and bringing about riots, stride, Rick,
shouldn't this be "strife"? Please check quote. turmoil,
and even death."

In the Dead of the Night

The time: Just after midnight

The date: June 12, 1963

The place: A quiet, moonlit, suburban street on the
outskirts of Jackson

The threat: A lone gunman crouching behind a clump
of honeysuckle vines

The target: NAACP State Field Secretary Medgar Evers

The gunman lifts the thirty-ought-six, high-powered
Enfield hunting rifle to his shoulder and places a squint-
ing eye to its six-power telescopic sight. Evers pulls his
blue 1962 Oldsmobile into the driveway of the ranch-style
house at 2332 Guyness Street. He opens the car door and
steps out holding a stack of T-shirts emblazed with the
slogan "Jim Crow Must Go." The events of the next hour
will change history.

—o

On that fateful night, Evers was returning home from a series of NAACP functions. He had updated his colleagues on the protest demonstrations shaking the state's capital city and had watched President Kennedy make a televised address to the nation, announcing plans to push new civil rights legislation in Congress, urging citizens to embrace tolerance and understanding over prejudice and hatred.

For his part, Evers had been prodding his NAACP colleagues to move beyond their courtroom arguments and economic boycotts to embrace the new, direct-action protests employed by student activists. His support of those tactics had led to a series of student marches and sit-ins in Jackson that spring, which had spurred more than 700 arrests and generated intense media coverage. Once dubbed a "quiet integrationist" by the *New York Times,* he was now being called a dangerous radical by the segregationist press at home. His high profile was also prompting hate mail, death threats, and attempts on his life. In a two-week period in late May and early June of 1963, a Molotov cocktail had been thrown into his carport and a speeding car had nearly run him down outside his office in Jackson.

Despite the dangers, Evers pressed forward. The principles of doing the right thing in the face of hardship had been impressed upon him by his parents during his childhood in the mill town of Decatur, Mississippi, in the 1920s and '30s. The hardships of life in a small, segregated town had included the day-to-day indignities of second-class citizenship and the hoots and howls of white hooligans who roamed the streets on weekends tossing firecrackers at black children. Evers dropped out of school in the 11th grade to join the Army and fight in World War II. On the battlefields of Europe he fought the Nazis—the ultimate white supremacists—learning that the defense of freedom carried the risk of death. Off the battlefields in Europe, he dated a white woman, realizing that racial segregation was not a universal reality. After returning home to Decatur, he tried to register to vote, only to be roughed up by a white mob. He vowed to make a difference.

Evers finished high school and took a degree in business administration at Alcorn A & M College. Setting out to prove that an African American could succeed in the Deep South, Evers took a job selling insurance for the black-owned Magnolia Mutual Life Insurance Company. Realizing the futility of pedaling life insurance policies to poor black dirt farmers who could barely afford food and shelter for their families, he put away the insurance policies and began handing out application forms for the NAACP. In the early 1950s, he started writing reports for the organization, chronicling the deplorable state of Negro schools and the prevalence of Klan violence. In 1954 he was named the organization's first Mississippi field secretary. In that role, he logged thousands of miles driving the state's two-lane highways and two-rut dirt roads, investigating lynchings, voter intimidation, and rampant discrimination.

—o

Naturally Evers had long been a subject of keen interest to the Commission. In his first years on the job, special operative T1 launched a basic background check on Evers, and agent Zack Van Landingham tracked his movements. Van Landingham seriously underestimated the quiet and introspective activist, filing a report that predicted Evers would fail to connect with grassroots activists because "he is a weak character and a coward" afraid to put himself "at forefront or in a position that would place him in danger of bodily harm." Before long Van Landingham was compiling extensive, 6- to 12-page memos on Evers's relentless activism, building an extensive dossier under the subject heading "Medgar Evers: Integration Agitator." The file included Evers's military records, college transcripts, car registration, and even the birth certificates of his children.

Van Landingham even chronicled Evers's attacks on the Commission. In a report on an NAACP meeting, the agent noted: "Evers spoke regarding the State Sovereignty Commission and mentioned my name as receiving reports from Negro informants all over the state."

In fact, the Commission's confidential informants had tracked the field secretary's movements for years.

And working in tandem with the Jackson City Police, they were closely monitoring his actions lin the spring of 1963, as picket lines and sit ins disrupted the daily flow of events in the state's capital city.

In May 1963 Commission agents intercepted a letter that Evers wrote to supporters and placed it in his investigative file. "The NAACP is determined to put an end to all forms of radical segregation in Jackson," Evers wrote. "To accomplish this we shall use all lawful means of protests—picketing, marches, mass mailings, litigation, and whatever other lawful means we deem necessary."

At another point Evers directly challenged the white power structure, going over their heads to appeal to ordinary citizens. "We believe that there are white Mississippians who want to go forward on the race question. Their religion tells them there is something wrong with the old system. Their sense of justice and fair play sends them the same message. But whether Jackson and the state choose to change or not, the years of change are upon us."

—o

Things never would be the same after June 12, 1963. Just after midnight, after stepping out of the car with the bundle of "Jim Crow Must Go" T-shirts, Evers walked up his driveway with his door key in hand. His wife, Myrlie, was watching television in the bedroom, their three children nestled on the bed with her. As Medger Evers walked toward the front door, the gunman in the shadows squeezed the trigger. The shot rang out, breaking the silence. The bullet ripped through Evers's back below his right shoulder blade, through a window, and through a wall inside the house. As Evers crawled to his front porch, blood pouring from his body, his keys still in hand, Myrlie ran out, horrified. Their children had taken cover under their beds as their parents had taught them to do at the sound of gunshots. They ran out a few minutes later to see their father lying in a pool of blood. Myrlie rushed back inside and called the police. Her husband was rushed to the hospital but died 50 minutes later.

—o

The next morning Jackson City Police scoured the crime scene. Sergeant O. M. Luke found the thirty-ought-six rifle in a honeysuckle vine less than 400 feet from Evers's driveway. Jackson Police Captain Ralph Hargrove photographed the scene and brought the rifle back to his office to examine. Meticulously dusting the rifle for prints, a single index finger print on the scope "practically jumped up." Hargrove sent the print to FBI, which matched it with a print in a military file belonging to Byron de la Beckwith, a founding member of the White Citizens' Council and Klansman from Greenville. It turned out that de la Beckwith also drove a white Plymouth Valiant, the same color and make of car seen prowling Evers's neighborhood the day of the murder.

De la Beckwith was not completely unknown to the Commission. Deep in its secret files was a letter he had written in 1957 to then Governor Coleman asking for a job with the segregation watchdogs. In the letter de la Beckwith listed his qualifications: "Expert with a pistol, good with a rifle and fair with a shotgun—and —RABID ON THE SUBJECT OF SEGREGATION! I therefore request that you select me, among many, as one who will tear the mask from the face of the NAACP and forever rid this fair land of the DISEASE OF INTEGRATION with which it is plagued with." He wasn't hired.

—o

As the civil rights community mourned, tragedy struck again. An outcry was building in the North over the worsening condition of Clyde Kennard, still serving a seven-year sentence at Parchman on trumped-up charges of being an accomplice to theft of five bags of chicken feed. With cancer ravishing Kennard's body, Barnett finally released him to avoid a public relations nightmare of allowing a political prisoner to die in custody. Two months after returning to Chicago, on the Fourth of July of 1963, Clyde Kennard died of cancer. Ironically Evers had spoken out on Kennard's behalf for years. Now both men were gone.

—o

Amid the gloom, the state came under intense pressure to bring Evers's killer to justice. In late June, de la

Beckwith was arrested and charged with murder. Under police questioning, de la Beckwith claimed that his rifle had been stolen before the shooting. He also claimed to be playing cards with friends on the night of the murder. Two of those friends turned out be police officers, who backed up his alibi in court. During the high-profile trial, the defendant—clad in a linen suit, monogrammed shirt, and French cuffs—appeared cocky and unrepentant. During breaks in the proceedings, he strutted around the courtroom, offering cigars to the prosecutor, chatting cotton prices with farmers in the gallery, whispering racist quotes to reporters. As the White Citizens' Council raised funds for his defense, de la Beckwith became a poster boy for racial hatred. In the end, the all-white jury could not agree upon a verdict, and a mistrial was declared.

Certain that de la Beckwith was guilty, state prosecutors prepared for a retrial. The de la Beckwith defense team knew that their best hope was to seat another jury incapable of reaching a unanimous guilty verdict. This would force the court to set de la Beckwith free. At that point defense attorney Stanny Stanners called Commission investigator Andy Hopkins with a highly unusual request. He asked Hopkins to screen 11 prospective jurors. Hopkins, an FBI-trained investigator, was uneasy, questioning the ethics of intervening on behalf of the defense in the state prosecution of a high-profile murder case. He asked his Commission superiors for permission to intervene in the case and got the go-ahead. The only caveat: avoid direct, personal contact with prospective jurors.

Hopkins called the prospective jurors' employers and associates and compiled a report on their work histories and affiliations, noting their involvement in groups like the White Citizens' Council. Next to one man's name the agent scrawled "believed to be Jewish" (that prospective juror was dismissed), and next to others he wrote "fair and impartial" (those were seated). In the end, the all-white, all-male, all-Protestant jury deadlocked, and de la Beckwith went free—to brag at Klan rallies of getting away with murder. Given his ability to postpone justice, he was tagged with the nickname Delay Beckwith.

CHAPTER 13

The Secret Benefactor

As the Evers trial drama played out, another story was
unfolding on the national stage. President Kennedy was
pushing Congress to pass sweeping civil rights legislation
to bar segregation in public places and strengthen voting
rights. Southern lawmakers and Northern conserva-
tives were mounting fierce opposition to the bill, and an
effective anti–civil rights lobbying campaign was chip-
ping away at support, too. Few on the national political
scene realized the anti–civil rights campaign was being
waged by a secretive state segregationist agency in far-off
Mississippi. The Commission had gone national.

Commission Public Relations Chief Erle Johnston ck
spelling had been promoted to director and was dem-
onstrating a knack for high-level political maneuvering.
In the summer of '63, Johnston traveled to Washington,
D.C., to take part in a hush-hush conference "to lay
plans for an organized effort to defeat the new Kennedy

civil rights program." In the weeks to come, Johnston, Sovereignty Commission attorney John Satterfield, and several prominent conservative political leaders formed the Coordinating Committee for Fundamental American Freedoms, a national lobbying organization dedicated to defeating the Kennedy bill. Operating from a plush suite of offices overlooking congressional staff buildings on Capitol Hill, the group pumped out speeches, press releases, newspaper ads, and television spots denouncing the bill, falsely claiming it would require employers to replace white workers with black workers, destroy the national budget, and lead to socialism. The campaign became the most costly lobbying effort of its day.

The lobbying program was funded primarily by the Commission, which had raised private donations in Mississippi and tapped its own budget to jump-start the effort. In addition, it had taken in $209,010 in private donations (more than $3.2 million in today's money) from an anonymous, out-of-state donor.

The secret benefactor was a wealthy white supremacist from New York named Wickliffe Preston Draper, who had also funded social experiments aimed at breeding a white superrace and research into the prospects of resettling blacks in Africa. How frightening were Draper and his associates? Prior to World War II, Draper attended a conference in Berlin and befriended German interior minister Wilhelm Frick, who ended up being hanged for crimes against humanity after the war. At the conference, Draper's travel companion and colleague Dr. Clarence Campbell sympathized with the Germans on the issue of race and ethnicity. "The differences between the Jew and the Aryan," he said, "are as insurmountable as that between black and white."

During the legislative battle over the Kennedy bill, Draper's generosity was kept under wraps. As far as the segregationists were concerned, the public had no need to know that the anti–civil rights lobby was being bank-rolled by a white supremacist and Nazi sympathizer and that his money had been routed through a segregationist spy agency to the lobbying campaign. Then came the shocking assassination of President Kennedy in Dallas on November 22, 1963. Would this end the push for a new civil rights bill? The answer turned out to be no. Five days after the assassination, President Johnson urged a joint session of Congress to pay homage to the fallen leader by passing the Civil Rights Act of 1964. The legis-lative battle raged on.

CHAPTER 14

Agent X

A tall, well-dressed, black man strides with confidence down the hallway of the Masonic Temple in the heart of the bustling "colored section" of Jackson, Mississippi, in March of 1964. He stops at a door leading to the large meeting room, waits for a nod from a man standing guard, and takes a seat in the spectators' gallery. Scanning the faces of the men and women sitting at the meeting table in the center of the room, he recognizes a virtual Who's Who of the state's civil rights leadership, including the highest-ranking leaders of the NAACP and the Student Non-violent Coordinating Committee (SNCC). The unassuming spectator listens intently. No one in the room suspects that the seemingly innocuous visitor has his own agenda. Far from being a sympathizer with the cause, he is actually a private detective, being paid to keep tabs on the civil rights crusaders for the segregationist state.

After the meeting, the private eye reports to his superiors at the Day Detective Agency in Jackson, providing a synopsis of the meeting and a document marked "Confidential: Mississippi Freedom Summer." The Day detectives will supply a full report to their prized client, the Mississippi State Sovereignty Commission. The report—single-spaced on plain white paper—will bear the telltale mark of a hand-scrawled X with a circle around it—the sign that it originated with a top secret, black informant code-named Agent X.

—o

The report from Agent X described plans for an extensive voter registration campaign to be carried out across the state over the coming summer. The project would link hundreds—perhaps even thousands—of mostly white college students from the North with dozens of black freedom workers from Mississippi. Three major civil rights organizations—the NAACP, SNCC, and CORE— would execute the campaign under the umbrella of the Council of Federated Organizations (COFO).

The document attached to the report said that more than 2,000 students, teachers, nurses, and legal advisors would form a "Peace Corps–type operation" designed to transform race relations in the state. The volunteers would set up Freedom Schools to teach reading and writing to black children and teens and establish community centers to provide adult literacy classes and vocational training programs to adults. Volunteers would also prepare thousands of blacks to register to vote for the first time and lay the groundwork for black candidates to run for public office.

"The program of voter registration and political organization will attempt to change the fundamental structure of political and economic activity in Mississippi," the report stated.

As plans for Freedom Summer developed, Agent X worked through his bosses at the Day Detective Agency to continue to feed intelligence to the Commission, revealing the organizers' plans to prepare "Negros to run for the United States Congress." "It appears now that one of the main purposes of the proposed statewide voter registration campaign is directed to this end," one report stated. The infiltrator considered no piece of intelligence insignificant, even reporting plans for a "completely integrated" folk concert starring singer Joan Baez on April 5, 1964, at Tougaloo College to drum up interest in the summer offensive.

As Freedom Summer grew closer, Agent X scored another coup. He persuaded the COFO leadership to put him on the staff. "After a few interviews," he reported, "I was offered a position." Upon gaining the trust of the COFO staff, he began searching the office for confidential reports that could reveal the latest plans. The clever infiltrator patiently awaited his chance to intercept the documents. On June 2, he told his handlers, "I decided it would be better to wait another day before picking up this literature."

At an opportune moment, he secretly copied the applications of student activists accepted into the Freedom Summer program. He passed the names, addresses, license numbers, and photographs on to the Commission.

As the clock continued to tick, Agent X wrangled an invitation to an extensive training seminar for several hundred student activists to be held at the Western College for Women in Oxford, Ohio, on June 16, 1964. On that date, Director Johnston was informed that "X is departing this date for Oxford, Ohio, with wife and will forward reports to a blind P.O. Box here in Jackson and make periodic telephone reports on activities."

Upon arriving on the campus on June 17, X seamlessly blended into sessions preparing the student activists for the danger ahead. Posing as one of the few black activists from Mississippi, he gained access to sessions on registering voters, dealing with police brutality, forming freedom schools, and registering voters.

During one session his friend R. Jess Brown, a black lawyer from Jackson, told the students: "Now get this in your heads and remember what I am going to say. They—the white folk, the police, the state police—they are all waiting for you. They are looking for you. They are ready. They are armed. They know some of your names and your descriptions even now, even before you get to Mississippi."

Naturally, Agent X knew the full truth behind the statement of his unsuspecting friend. He was one of the operatives making sure that it was true. He had supplied the Commission with extensive information on the Freedom Summer throughout that spring and filed more extensive reports through his 11 days at the training seminar. He revealed the names, descriptions and destinations of key activists, the role to be played by volunteer lawyers, the plans of reporters covering the initiative, and the mounting fears of students destined for hostile territory.

—o

All the while X was feeding the pipeline, the Commission staff had been working diligently to prepare for the "invasion." Commission Agent Tom Scarborough set up meetings across the state to prepare public officials and civic leaders for the onslaught of Northern college students. "The purpose of these meetings has been to organize the city and county officials to work in a coordinated unit to handle the racial agitators who have promised to invade Mississippi this summer," Scarborough reported. In Lafayette County, Scarborough warned community leaders that the invasion would be led by "communists, sex perverts, odd balls, and do-gooders."

Commission agents also set out to visit sheriff's offices in all 82 counties to prepare law enforcement officers for potential trouble. The agents provided police with a summary of 19 state laws that could be used to arrest or detain troublemakers. Their goal was to strengthen the hand of county sheriff's offices statewide, which had also been fortified with hundreds of newly deputized auxiliary officers. The police were gearing up for a virtual war with the "outside agitators."

—o

As the Commission fueled the fevered preparations, a new development arose. Agent Andy Hopkins had been investigating the intense competition for recruits between violent new factions of the Klan. One night shots were fired into Hopkins's house and Klan literature was left in his yard. It appeared that the resurgent Klan was gearing up for war, too. The new Klan was so extreme that it was ready to take on the Commission itself—on top of their common enemy—in defense of white rule.

The wild swirl of events was cascading out of the control of a state leadership that had changed dramatically over the past six months. Former Lieutenant Governor Paul Johnson had been elected to succeed his mentor Ross Barnett, running on the slogan "Stand Tall with Paul," reminding voters of his stand in the schoolhouse door at Ole Miss. Commission Director Erle Johnston was advising the new governor on the state's preparations for Freedom Summer. But as the summer program drew close, Johnston informed his boss of "secret organizations of white people, whose mission apparently is to take laws into their own hands."

In fact, the newly formed and violent White Knights of the Ku Klux Klan were entering dozens of recruits in the newly formed auxiliary police units. These Klansman would not wear hoods and robes to confront the "invaders" but badges and state-issued firearms. As Freedom Summer approached, the imperial wizard of the White Knights, Sam Bowers, told his followers: "The first contact with the troops of the enemy in the street should be as legally deputized law enforcement officers."

Marked Men

Michael Schwerner, Andrew Goodman, and James Cheney were at the Freedom Summer training seminar in Ohio, too. The three young activists listened to lectures, attended workshops, and sang freedom songs, never imagining that a black segregationist spy was watching and listening. On June 20, 1964, the three climbed into their COFO-issued, blue 1963 Ford Fairlane station wagon and set out for the Mt. Zion Methodist Church in Neshoba County, Mississippi, which had been doused with kerosene and set ablaze by Klansmen three nights before. The activists wanted to help the congregation rebuild the church and use it as a Freedom School.

—o

Like many of the Freedom Summer volunteers, Schwerner, Goodman, and Cheney were in their 20s, idealistic, and committed, but they hailed from vastly different backgrounds.

Michael "Mickey" Schwerner was 24, white, college-educated, and married. He was the son of a successful businessman and a high school biology teacher from New York. Mickey sported a trademark goatee and loved sports, rock music, poker, and W. C. Fields. In his application to serve as a CORE organizer, Schwerner vowed to spend the rest of his life working toward an integrated society. He had spent the previous summer registering voters in Meridian, Mississippi.

Andrew Goodman was a 20-year-old white graduate of a liberal, private high school in New York, who had gone on to study at Queens College. He hailed from an affluent, politically connected family that owned a share of the left-leaning Pacifica radio network. Goodman had a flair for music and acting. He felt that a summer of civil rights work in Mississippi would extend his horizons beyond his privileged background.

James Cheney was a 21-year-old poor, black native of Meridian, Mississippi. His mother cleaned houses for white families, and his father worked construction jobs as a plasterer before he left the family. As James matured, he recognized the depth of discrimination in his hometown and saw civil rights work as a route out.

—o

On the afternoon of June 21, 1964, Schwerner, Goodman, and Cheney rolled into Neshoba County en route to the ruins of the Mt. Zion Methodist Church. Schwerner was at the wheel of the station wagon, license number H 25503. The car was already on a watch list at the Neshoba County sheriff's office. In the wild swirl of events leading up to Freedom Summer, the Commission had sent the information to law enforcement across the state, and the White Citizens' Council had picked it up and circulated it as well. Schwerner was particularly well known to the authorities, given his work registering voters in Meridian the year before. Schwerner was also well known to the White Knights of the Ku Klux Klan, whose leaders nicknamed him "Goatee" and targeted him for death.

At about 4 p.m., Neshoba County Deputy Sheriff Cecil Price pulled over the car. Price arrested Schwerner for speeding and took all three to the jail in nearby Philadelphia. As the men sat in their cells, armed Klansman began gathering outside. At about 10:30 p.m., the police released the three, with the Klansman still milling on the street. As the activists climbed back into their car and headed out of town, Deputy Price followed in a squad car. The Klansmen were close behind.

The next day the activists' burned-out station wagon was found in the Bogue Chitto Swamp outside Philadelphia. There was no sign of the three men. Their disappearance spurred an international media frenzy and a massive search. Even President Johnson got involved, consoling the activists' families and ordering FBI Director J. Edgar Hoover to lead the search. The President also

ordered Hoover to take down the Mississippi Klan—once
and for all.

—o

Naturally the Commission had it covered on all sides.
Just before his departure from the Ohio training seminar,
Agent X had reported that student activists had gotten
word of the disappearances and were being flooded
with phone calls and telegrams from their relatives
urging them to withdraw from the project. Commission
agent Andy Hopkins had rushed to Philadelphia to
monitor events and shadow the FBI. A former FBI man
himself, Hopkins reported that the town was abuzz with
rumors that "these subjects met with foul play either
while in custody of the sheriff or shortly after their
release." A few days later Hopkins reported more talk
around town: "There are rumors that there is a KKK in
Philadelphia and some prominent citizens are members
of the Klan." Despite the talk, Hopkins maintained the
view of many locals, who insisted the incident was a
publicity stunt designed by COFO to grab headlines.
Hopkins also complained that FBI agents were elbowing
state investigators out of the probe and strong-arming
suspects for information. A couple of weeks into the
search, however, Hopkins conceded that the FBI tactics
were getting results, particularly their round-the-clock
surveillance of suspected Klansmen and their willingness
to dole out tens of thousands of dollars for information.

The search for the missing men went on for six weeks. The FBI dragged swamps and searched woods. The Mississippi Highway Patrol kept watch across the state in the event the missing men showed up unexpectedly. The Jackson *Clarion Ledger* speculated that the three "agitators" were probably in "Cuba or another Communist area awaiting their next task." Then the speculation ended. On August 4, 1964, 44 days after the civil rights workers were last seen alive, FBI agents dug up their bodies, buried deep into an earthen dam. Commission agent Hopkins supplied his bosses with a hand-drawn map showing the burial site, noting that the bodies were discovered 14 feet down.

The tragic discovery put a worldwide spotlight on Klan violence in Mississippi. But as the headlines and television reports circled the globe, the violence and reprisals continued in the Magnolia State. Over the course of the summer, more than 40 black churches were burned and hundreds of activists were jailed. For their part, the Freedom Summer volunteers registered 1,600 new black voters, opened 37 Freedom Schools, and organized a bi-racial slate of candidates to challenge the all-white Democratic Party regulars at the national convention that fall. The accomplishments were less grand than originally envisioned but significant nonetheless. The tide was turning.

The Magnolia Curtain

During that pivotal summer another historic event
loosened the segregationists' hold on power. Following a
filibuster by Southern senators, Congress passed the Civil
Rights Act of 1964—a fitting tribute to the late President
Kennedy and a watershed moment in the history of
the civil rights movement. President Johnson signed
the bill as part of his program for a "Great Society," a
vision of a nation free of widespread poverty, ignorance,
and injustice. The new law prohibited segregation in
places serving the general public, including restaurants,
hotels, motels, playgrounds, and swimming pools. Even
more important, it allowed the federal government to
cut off funds to any state-supported program found to
be practicing racial discrimination, including schools,
hospitals, defense plants, and research labs. The threat
of losing tens of millions of dollars in U.S. government
funding was not lost on embattled state officials, who

were finally rethinking their determination to maintain segregation "at all costs."

It was about then that Ole Miss history professor James Silver revealed to the nation the depth of the state's disdain of dissent, its censorship of books, its control of the media, and its use of secret agents to undercut civil rights. In his book *Mississippi: The Closed Society,* Silver described a state that operated more like a totalitarian police regime than a part of the modern United States of America. Silver knew firsthand of the Commission's methods through its repeated efforts to get him fired from Ole Miss. With public interest in Mississippi peaking in the wake of Freedom Summer, the book became a bestseller, adding to the national pressure on the state to change its ways.

Given those pressures, the snarl of the segregationists began to ease. One of the first signs of change came from Governor Paul Johnson, who, during his campaign, had referred to the NAACP as the National Association of Apes, Coons, Niggers, and Possums. Now he was pledging to put an end to the state's support for white racism. "We are not going to be the pushing boy for that element ever again," he said. "We built the dog house we now find ourselves in." Meantime, the Klan was being dismantled by the FBI, and membership in the White Citizens' Council was waning, as the white middle class distanced itself from violence. The Magnolia Curtain was lifting, but a serious question remained: Could the Commission change?

"Destroy this Directive"

By 1965, Commission Director Erle Johnston was describing his segregation watchdogs as a cadre of "racial troubleshooters," a problem-solving liaison between the white community and the black community. Seeking to rise above the reputation of a "super-snooping operation," Johnston told white civic groups the Commission was now dedicated to negotiating solutions to disputes, intervening early to prevent misunderstandings and flare ups. In fact Johnston did take steps to curb the excesses of the operation. He finally cut off payments to the White Citizens' Council and became an informant to the FBI, providing valuable information for its crackdown on the Klan.

Nevertheless, the agency never really abandoned its segregationist mission—as if racism had been infused in its DNA. While publicly touting the agency as a "troubleshooter," Johnston continued to play the role as the hidden protector of white rule. At one point he fired off a letter to a state recreation official recommending "closing swimming pools at the end of this summer" rather than allowing black and white children to swim together in integrated pools. His advice was not heeded. He also advised admissions officers at Southern Mississippi College to force a black applicant to drop his application for admission by threatening to expose the student's sexual preference. "We have information that you are a homosexual," Johnston wrote. "If you change your mind about enrolling at an all-white university we will say no more about it. If you persist in your application, we will give this information to the press and Justice Department." The prospective student did not enroll.

That year Johnston also issued one of his most telling directives. He ordered agents to destroy documents in the Commission files. His confidential memo instructed his spies to purge their files of investigative reports that suggested illegal activity, particularly reports suggesting interference with the voter registration process. Johnston went on to direct agents to write future reports with code words and phrases to obscure the nature of the investigations. For example, investigative reports were to refer to voting registration volunteers as "subversives," insulating the agents from charges of tampering with the vote. His memo concluded: "Except for a copy being sent to the governor's office, no record of these directions will remain in our files. As soon as you have familiarized yourself with the contents, please destroy this directive." The agents destroyed the incriminating files but forgot to destroy Johnston's memo.

By 1966 Johnston was growing weary, beaten down by criticism from both sides of the racial divide. He tried unsuccessfully to persuade his superiors to change the name of the Commission to the Mississippi State Information Agency and recast it as a modern public relations outlet. But too many powerful politicians wanted the watchdog to remain on the job. By 1967 he was arguing that the Commission had "outlived its usefulness" and was "ready for the grave." Finally, in November 1967, he announced his resignation. The State Legislature thanked him for his service but refused to shut down the operation, replacing him with a former FBI agent and maintaining a skeleton staff.

Through the late '60s, the scaled-back agency monitored school desegregation, kept tabs on anti–Vietnam War protestors, and snooped on a couple of black power groups. By the early '70s, the powerful politicians on the Commission's governing board routinely skipped meetings, proposals to eliminate its budget came and went, and the staff was reduced to infiltrating rock concerts to spy on hippies. By the summer of 1973, the agency's obituary was finally being written, with the *Memphis Commercial Appeal* reporting that Mississippi's "Ole Watchdog is Barking for its Life."

On July 1, 1973, the Commission staff was released, its office closed, and its records locked. Four years later the state legislature finally abolished the law that had created the Commission back in 1956.

This chapter of history was finally over. The Commission was abolished, the Citizens Council marginalized, and the Klan tamed. The Civil Rights Act and Voting Rights Act were the law of the land. The march toward equality and justice had picked up its pace. But the questioned remain: Could Mississippi really change over time?

In the course of researching this book, I traveled across the state contemplating that question and searching for answers. From the vast cotton fields and moss-draped bayous of the delta to the hurricane-racked homes and glittering casinos on the Gulf Coast to the state offices and streets of Jackson, I witnessed the progress that has been made since the rule of the segregationists, when the creed of white supremacy stood as bedrock and the code of racial separation was enforced with an iron fist. The "whites only" signs are long gone from the café windows, and the storefront offices that once housed White Citizens' Council chapters have long been converted into restaurants and gift shops. Today, legions of black and white children attend school together and long lines of black and white voters line up at the polls on election day. Racial violence is a discussion topic for history students at Ole Miss rather than a frightening reality of life on that once war-torn campus.

I also saw the ghosts of the past lurking behind the signs of progress. The names of segregationist politicians are proudly etched into the granite of public buildings. Their official biographies are often cleansed of the cold, hard truth of a bygone era that many would prefer to forget. Those ghosts whisper that principles of the past are still with us and remind us that history can always return as the future.

In fact there is evidence that the bad old days are poised for a comeback. For the past two decades, public schools have been gradually resegregating as federal and state courts back off enforcement of integration laws and legislatures sidestep the issue. New white-is-right pressure groups have resurrected the concepts of the long-defunct White Citizens Council, targeting a new generation of potential race warriors on the Internet. The history of the civil rights movement is still largely unknown to adults and children—not only in Mississippi but across much of the nation.

My advice is that everyone read the Commission files, with their chilling investigative reports on private citizens and their underhanded tactics for maintaining the status quo. In the end, the files are an important reminder of the dangers of unchecked power and the reckless disregard for individual rights. And while those files reflect the excesses of the powerful, they also reveal the strength of the people who refused to play the role of the powerless. As the investigative reports show, many of the true civil rights heroes of the era were ordinary folks who hailed from the small towns and clapboard shacks of the Magnolia State, who carried on their struggle to bring down segregation and discrimination with the constant shadow of the state looming over them. Their names—categorized in the files as race agitators, subversives and communists—live on as champions of the most powerful democratic movement in our history.

Epilogue

What Happened Next

The Commission Files: The end of the Commission started a heated debate over the fate of the six locked file cabinets of secret papers that had been removed from the office and stored in an underground vault. Resisting calls from lawmakers to destroy the files altogether, the legislature voted to keep the documents sealed for another 50 years, until July 1, 2027. The American Civil Liberties Union filed suit demanding the documents be opened to the public without delay. The courts finally ordered the files to be made public, and their release in 1998 revealed the extent of the secret enterprise.

The FBI: Director J. Edgar Hoover carried out his orders to defuse Klan violence in Mississippi but proved no friend to the civil rights movement. By the mid-1960s Hoover was pressing ahead with COINTELPRO—a massive federal spying operation targeting civil rights advocates, anti-war groups, and alleged Communists. The bureau's use of electronic eavesdropping, masterful sabotage, and extensive infiltration took the art of domestic spying to a dangerous new level.

Agent X: The Day Detective Agency operated a string of black agents for the Commission. The reports were filed under the code name Informant X to protect the identity of the operatives. Following the release of the Commission papers, civil rights activists studied the files with one question in mind: Who was at the meetings and encounters that ended up in those reports to the Commission? A number of activists pointed to R. L. Bolden, who had attended infiltrated meetings, worked on compromised campaigns, and been at the scene of the Freedom Summer training seminars in Ohio. In an interview for this book, Bolden conceded that he worked with the Day Agency and admitted that he provided his bosses with details of civil rights meetings. He insisted the information he passed along was public, claiming there were no secrets in the wide-open civil rights movement. Acknowledging that the Day Agency may have passed his information onto the Commission, he added, "I was not the only one."

Erle Johnston After retiring from the Commission, Johnston returned to his hometown, edited his weekly

newspaper, and authored a number of books, including
a reminiscence of segregationist Governor Ross Barnett
under the title *I Rolled with Ross*. Through the years,
Johnston seemed conflicted between the romance of
operating near the height of state power and the shame
of doing the bidding of the white power structure.
Following the release of the files, Johnston came under
criticism for the agency's excesses, and his claims of
being a "practical segregationist" and "troubleshooter"
failed to dissuade his detractors. He sat on a board dedicated to the preservation of historic papers for Tugaloo
College, which he once spied on. He died in 1995.

J. P. Coleman: After leaving the governor's office,
Coleman went on to a distinguished career in government. Driven by a passion for public service, he ran for
and won a seat in the state legislature in 1960 and was
appointed a federal judge in 1965. He served on the
federal court for 16 years. His legacy would always be
compromised by the stroke of his pen that created the
Sovereignty Commission. He died in 1991.

Aaron Henry: Henry persevered in his fight for integration and voting rights, serving as a coalition builder and
leader. He was elected to the Mississippi Legislature in
1982 and served until 1996. He died in 1997.

Clyde Kennard: After succumbing to cancer in 1963, Kennard's attempt to integrate Mississippi Southern College was reduced to a footnote in civil rights history. But then students at Lincolnshire High School in Illinois, working with the Center for Wrongful Convictions at Northwestern University, persuaded Kennard's accuser to recant the testimony that had led to Kennard's conviction as an accomplice to the theft of five bags of chicken feed. In 2006 a judge in the same courtroom where Kennard had been found guilty back in 1960, vacated his conviction. In addition, a building has been named in his honor at the University of Southern Mississippi, formerly Mississippi Southern College.

Ross Barnett: After leaving the governor's office in 1964, Barnett suffered a decline in popularity as word of his secret dealings with the Kennedys spread. He failed in a second bid for the governor's office and faded from public view. He was reduced to speaking at white supremacist gatherings and playing accordion and telling stories at county fairs. He died in 1987.

James Meredith: After graduating from Ole Miss, Meredith was shot while leading a "March Against Fear" from Memphis to Jackson in 1966. Dr. Martin Luther King and other civil rights leaders continued the march for him, and Meredith recovered from his wounds and rejoined the trek. Years later, in a dramatic shift, Meredith became a stockbroker, a member of the Republican Party, and a staff member of arch conservative Senator Jesse Helms, claiming that liberal Democrats were the greatest enemies of African Americans. He also wrote an 11-volume history of Mississippi. In 1997 he donated his personal papers to Ole Miss.

Byron de la Beckwith: After walking away free from two trials in the shooting death of Medgar Evers, "Delay Beckwith" went on to play a leadership role in white supremacist groups. In 1994, de la Beckwith was retried for the murder of Medgar Evers amid revelations that the Commission had intervened for the defense during the second trial. This time a jury of eight blacks and four whites found him guilty, and a judge sentenced him to life at Parchman penitentiary. He died in prison in 2001.

Percy Greene: Greene finally sold his newspaper and retired, scorned as a sellout by many in the black community. As activist Fred Clark recalled: "They were paying him for those articles that he would write about black people...He was wearing fine suits, smoking the best cigars, but deep down inside people around him didn't like him because of how he was getting his money, off the blood of the black people. But he had suffered himself and just didn't see no light or no hope at the end of the tunnel."

Credits

Index

Index